797,885 Books
are available to read at

Forgotten Books

www.ForgottenBooks.com

Forgotten Books' App
Available for mobile, tablet & eReader

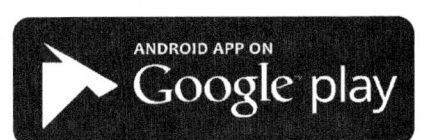

ISBN 978-1-330-14292-9
PIBN 10036316

This book is a reproduction of an important historical work. Forgotten Books uses state-of-the-art technology to digitally reconstruct the work, preserving the original format whilst repairing imperfections present in the aged copy. In rare cases, an imperfection in the original, such as a blemish or missing page, may be replicated in our edition. We do, however, repair the vast majority of imperfections successfully; any imperfections that remain are intentionally left to preserve the state of such historical works.

Forgotten Books is a registered trademark of FB &c Ltd.
Copyright © 2015 FB &c Ltd.
FB &c Ltd, Dalton House, 60 Windsor Avenue, London, SW19 2RR.
Company number 08720141. Registered in England and Wales.

For support please visit www.forgottenbooks.com

1 MONTH OF FREE READING

at

www.ForgottenBooks.com

By purchasing this book you are eligible for one month membership to ForgottenBooks.com, giving you unlimited access to our entire collection of over 700,000 titles via our web site and mobile apps.

To claim your free month visit:

www.forgottenbooks.com/free36316

* Offer is valid for 45 days from date of purchase. Terms and conditions apply.

English
Français
Deutsche
Italiano
Español
Português

www.forgottenbooks.com

Mythology Photography **Fiction**
Fishing Christianity **Art** Cooking
Essays Buddhism Freemasonry
Medicine **Biology** Music **Ancient Egypt** Evolution Carpentry Physics
Dance Geology **Mathematics** Fitness
Shakespeare **Folklore** Yoga Marketing
Confidence Immortality Biographies
Poetry **Psychology** Witchcraft
Electronics Chemistry History **Law**
Accounting **Philosophy** Anthropology
Alchemy Drama Quantum Mechanics
Atheism Sexual Health **Ancient History**
Entrepreneurship Languages Sport
Paleontology Needlework Islam
Metaphysics Investment Archaeology
Parenting Statistics Criminology
Motivational

PUBLISHERS' NOTE.

The following posthumous work by the late Rev. G. Oliver, D.D., so widely and deservedly known by his numerous Masonic writings, is printed *verbatim et literatim* from his hitherto unpublished MS.

The opinion of several distinguished Freemasons, competent to advise in such a matter, was, that the work should not be revised, added to, nor in any way altered. This opinion has been the more confidently acted upon, as the MS. bears evidence of having been very carefully revised by the Doctor's own hand, and there is his own statement to the effect, that both the plan and treatment of the book had been well matured.

London, *November* 1875.

TABLE OF CONTENTS.

	PAGE
PUBLISHERS' NOTE	v
PREFACE	ix

INTRODUCTION.

THE PYTHAGOREAN TRIANGLE EXPLAINED, WITH A DISSERTATION ON THE PECULIARITIES OF MASONIC NUMBER . . . 1

CHAPTER I.

THE MONAD OR POINT DISCUSSED AS THE ORIGIN OF ALL CALCULATION.

(The Point, Monad, Unity, or the NUMBER ONE) . . . 31

CHAPTER II.

THE DUAD OR LINE EXEMPLIFIED.

(The Line, Duad, Duality, or the NUMBER TWO) . . . 53

CHAPTER III.

ILLUSTRATION OF THE TRIAD OR SUPERFICE.

(The Superfice, or Equilateral Triangle, Triad, Ternary, or the NUMBER THREE) 77

CHAPTER IV.

PROGRESSIVE GENERATION OF THE TETRAD OR SOLID, REPRESENTING FIRE.

(The Solid, Tetrad, Quaternary, or the NUMBER FOUR) . 101

CHAPTER V.

GEOMETRICAL APPLICATION OF THE PENTAD OR PYRAMID, REPRESENTING WATER.

(The Pyramid, Pentad, Quincunx, or the NUMBER FIVE)   123

CHAPTER VI.

INFINITE DIVISIBILITY OF THE HEXAD OR DOUBLE TRIANGLE, REPRESENTING EARTH.

(The Double Triangle, Hexagon, Hexad, or the NUMBER SIX) 145

CHAPTER VII.

REMARKABLE PROPERTIES OF THE HEPTAD.

(The Heptagon, Heptad, Septenary, or the NUMBER SEVEN) 167

CHAPTER VIII.

MYSTERIOUS REFERENCES OF THE OGDOAD OR CUBE, REPRESENTING AIR.

(The Cube, Ogdoad, Octaedron, or the NUMBER EIGHT)   187

CHAPTER IX.

ANCIENT SUPERSTITIONS ATTACHED TO THE ENNEAD OR TRIPLE TRIANGLE.

(The Ennead, Triple Triangle, Nonagon, or the NUMBER NINE) 199

CHAPTER X.

THE PERFECT NATURE OF THE DECAD OR CIRCLE, AND THE APPLICATION OF THE DODECAEDRON AS A REPRESENTATION OF THE SYSTEM OF THE UNIVERSE.

(The Circle, Decad, Panteleia, or the NUMBER TEN)   219

PREFACE.

FREEMASONRY is a science, as every brother knows, whose Landmarks are theoretically unalterable, and whose peculiar rites and ordinances are pronounced to be the same yesterday, to-day, and for ever. But, alas! the failure of these conditions proves that Masonry is but a mere human institution after all. It would be easy to produce a host of altered Landmarks for the purpose of showing that no obsolete ceremony or antiquated observance has been able to hold its own against the electric agency of modern progress.

Accordingly, in tracing the science from the earliest period of its existence, we must prepare ourselves to meet with many changes which have periodically occurred in consequence of improvements and discoveries in the liberal arts, and the amelioration of manners and customs, as science progressed from ignorance to learning, and from a comparatively savage condition to its present palmy state of refinement and moral culture.

To look for a different result would be to expect impossibilities. Improvements in art, science, and civilisation, have a mutual dependence on each other. A change in the one will necessarily produce a modification of all. This is a truism that will not admit of contradiction or dispute. When we hear, therefore, of ancient, quaint phrases, whether in general literature or in Freemasonry, being swallowed up and lost in the undeviating march of scientific and moral improvement, and the substitution of others which are more in accordance with the usages of a polished era, we are not to be surprised at such occurrences, nor complain, as many worthy Masons of the old school are apt to do, of modern innovations; as if the institution were expected to stand still, and remain exempt from the inevitable law of mutation to which all human sciences are exposed.

Thus, for instance, the present race of Masons are ignorant of the reference to a Master Mason's clothing, as the fraternity understood it a hundred and fifty years ago, and would scarcely refrain from an incredulous smile when they are told that it consisted of "a yellow jacket and a pair of blue breeches." But this was simply a figurative expression to signify the Third Great Light, which was appropriated to the Master, as the instrument by the use of which he drew his designs on the "Trasel Board" as a direction for the workmen; the upper part being of polished brass, and its points blue steel. In like manner, several other peculiar phrases have become obsolete, and are now imperfectly understood; as in the instance of the "Broached Thurnel" for the apprentices to learn their work upon, connected with the Trasel Board and the Rough Ashlar—the triad having been changed to the Tracing Board, Rough Ashlar, and Perfect Ashlar.

Again, what Mason of the present day understands the meaning of IRAH, which our ancient brethren were so proud of? And indeed it has puzzled many accomplished Masons of modern times. Being associated with the second degree, it is believed by some to have referred to a person. But this exposition involves two hostile interpretations, neither of which may be correct; one party holding the opinion that it signified Hiram Abiff; and another that it had a mysterious reference to King James III., as he was designated by his followers; and if the latter interpretation be correct, it was probably one of the symbolical words of the Order introduced into Masonry by the Jesuits, to express Rediet (redeat, redibit) Ad Habenas (Hæreditatem); according to the anagrammatic form of reading by initials. This was the opinion of Schneider. Some interpret IRAH, יראה, to mean *Fear*, as the *fear of God;* while others take it to be ירה, *he has taught;* and lastly, it has been referred to the Temple, as who should say, HE HAS LAID THE FOUNDATION. *Utrum horum mavis accipe.*

Who knows anything at the present day about the obsolete degrees of the Link and Wrestle? They were formerly connected with the Ark and Mark, the latter having been recently revived; while the Ark, or, as the degree was denominated, the Royal Ark Mariners, is in abeyance, and seldom practised amongst the English Masons, although it bears a reference to a legitimate Masonic event.

A cowan, or listener, was a character extremely obnoxious to our predecessors, and is not in much more favour amongst ourselves; albeit their quaint method of punishing him, when detected, is now altogether unknown—*e.g.*, to place him under the eaves of a house in stormy weather until the water ran in at his shoulders and out at his knees. Hence the appellation of eavesdropper, and the origin of the cautionary exclamation, "It rains!" The modern treatment of a cowan is simply—contempt.

The three fixed lights, or windows, subsequently exchanged for our lesser luminaries, were explained one hundred and fifty years ago to signify "the three Persons, Father, Son, Holy Ghost;" and were used to find out the meridian, "when the sun leaves the south, and breaks in at the west window of the Lodge." While the "mossy bed," the ancient signs of disgust and recognition, as well as the primitive name of a Master Mason, are equally obscure at the present day; having been swept away, along with the original method of characterising chemical bodies by symbols, as being no longer necessary to the system. Even the Masonic cipher, of which our brethren of the last century were justly proud, is now in abeyance, if not obsolete, for it is considered by the English fraternity a useless appendage that may be well dispensed with.

In the formula of opening the Lodge before the union of *ancient* and *modern* Masons in 1813, it was announced by the chair that "all swearing, whispering, and unmannerly or profane conversation," were strictly prohibited during Lodge hours, under such penalty as "the Bylaws shall inflict or a majority think proper." And the reason publicly assigned for this prudent course was, "that the business of the Lodge being thus happily begun might be conducted with decency, and closed in harmony and brotherly love." This formula was discontinued at the abovementioned period, and a new form substituted, which brought the Christian tendency of the Order more prominently before the Lodge.

There are also some passages in the old lectures which the brethren once took for genuine Landmarks, that have long been disused. In the Entered Apprentice's Lecture, the following passage occurs: "What is the day for?—To see in. What is the night for?—To hear in. How blows the wind?—Due east and west." Again: "How long do you serve your master?—From Monday morning till Saturday night. How do you serve him?—With chalk, charcoal, and earthen pan, &c." When speaking in the Fellow Craft's degree of the elevation of the middle chamber, the door was technically said to be "so high that a cowan could not reach to stick a pin in." And the illuminated letter, by which it was distinguished, was said to denote "the Great Architect of the Universe, or Him that was taken up to the topmost pinnacle of the Holy Temple at Jerusalem."

As a counterpoise to the abandonment of this group of trivial observances by modern practice, many valuable additions were introduced in the revised lectures during the eighteenth century as matters of detail, which our more ancient brethren would have been proud to acknowledge as manifest improvements in the system. These were at length collected and embellished by Bro. W. Preston; and his Ritual formed the solid basis on which the Lodge of Reconciliation, in the year 1814, constructed the Union Lectures which are now used in the English Lodges. During these gradual improvements, the doctrine of MASONIC NUMBER slowly but certainly progressed in every successive formula, until it reached its acme, in the above-named year, by the introduction of all those scientific numeral phenomena which are deduced from a philosophical consideration of the PYTHAGOREAN TRIANGLE.

In the earlier rituals, Number is but incidentally alluded to. The degrees, steps, lights, ornaments, furniture, and jewels, &c., were arranged on the principle of the Triad; the cardinal virtues, with their appropriate signs and references, represented the tetrad, which, together with the five points of fellowship and the seven liberal sciences, appear to be all the numerical references which they contain; and they were not enlarged on or explained until Preston promulgated his Lectures under the sanction of the Grand Lodge. And here the numbers 3, 5, 7, and 11 are illustrated rather more in detail in his improved version of the Winding Staircase.

In the following pages, the doctrines and references which necessarily result from a minute consideration of the Science of Numbers, as enunciated in the Pythagorean Triangle, will be subjected to a scientific analysation; for it is a remarkable fact, that although the institution of Freemasonry is based upon it, we have no authorised lecture to illustrate its fundamental principles, or display its mysterious properties. At every step, we find a triad reference, but the reasons why this occurs are not satisfactorily explained. The monad, the duad, the triad, and the tetrad, meet us at every turn; and though these numbers constitute the foundation of all arithmetical calculations, the candidate is not fully instructed how they operate, or in what manner they ought to be applied.

A large portion of the Egyptian philosophy and religion seems to have been constructed almost wholly upon the science of numbers; and we are assured by Kircher (Œdip. Egypt., tom. ii. p. 2) that everything in nature was explained on this principle alone. The Pythagoreans had so high an opinion of it, that they considered it to be the origin of all things, and thought a knowledge of numbers to be equivalent to a knowledge of God. The founder of the sect received his instructions in this science from the Egyptian priests; who taught him that, while the monad possesses the nature of the efficient cause, the duad is merely a passive matter. A *point* corresponds with the monad, both being indivisible; and as the monad is the principle of numbers, so is the point of lines. A *line* corresponds with the duad, both being considered by transition. A line is length without breadth, extending between two points. A *superfice* corresponds with the triad, because in addition to the duad, length, it possesses a third property, viz., breadth; which is effected by setting down three points, two opposite, the third at the juncture of the lines made by the other two. A *solid* or cube represents the tetrad; for if we make three points in a triangular form, and set a fourth over them, we have a solid body in the form of a pyramid, which has three dimensions—length, and breadth, and thickness.

In expressing their opinion of the Regular or Platonic bodies, the followers of Pythagoras argued that the world was made by God "in thought, and not in time;" and that He commenced His work in fire and the fifth element; for there are five figures of solid bodies which are termed mathematical. *Earth* was made of a cube, *Fire* of a pyramid, *Air* of an octaedron, *Water* of an icosaedron, *the Sphere of the*

Universe of a dodecaedron. And the combinations of the monad, as the principle of all things, are thus deduced. From the monad came the indeterminate duad; from them came numbers; from numbers, points; from points, lines; from lines, superfices; from superfices, solids; from these, solid bodies whose elements are four, viz., fire, water, air, earth; of all of which, under various transmutations, the world consists.

Such dissertations, so far as they are applicable to the Science of Number, have received some attention in the revised Fellow Craft's Lecture of Dr Hemming, by an elucidation of the Pythagorean Triangle. The subject is one of surpassing interest to the Free and Accepted Mason, particularly if he be a lover of general Science. At my first initiation, I soon discovered the numerical peculiarity by which the Order is distinguished, and wondered that the Lectures contained such a meagre explanation of this extraordinary fact. Being somewhat addicted to mathematical studies, I took an intense interest in the pursuit, and, during a course of miscellaneous reading, made various collections on the subject of numbers, simple and compound, which I found invaluable when I became the Master of a Lodge.

True, I was sailing in the dark, without either compass or pilot, for the philosophy of Masonry was very imperfectly understood in those days. My researches, however, still made a gradual though slow progress, for what will not perseverance effect? Whatever I read contributed to my store, for there is no book so bad but some benefit may be derived from it by an industrious man, as the bee extracts honey from the poisonous flower; and even when I made no notes, I was steadily amassing materials for future use in the peculiar walk of Masonic literature which I was destined to pursue. It will readily be believed, that I had not the slightest intention of writing for the press at that early period of my career; for Masonic publications at the commencement of the present century were by no means in favour with the English Craft; and therefore, I threw my acquisitions together as they arose, simply for my own private reference, and without suspecting that they would ever appear in a printed form. But man proposes, and God disposes.

From these collections the following Treatise was drawn up. It has been several years in hand, and was not originally intended for publication; but in compliance with an urgent request which has been recently made upon me, I have allowed the manuscript to be put to press, in the hope that it will afford amusement and instruction to the assiduous Mason who consults its pages with the sober intention of improving his knowledge, by acquiring a store of additional facts which may assist his investigations into the more abstruse arcana of Masonic Numbers.

It has been well observed, that such speculations are by some considered as trifling and useless; but perhaps they judge too hastily; for few employments are more innocent, none more ingenious, nor, to those who have a taste for them, more amusing; and mathematical amusements sometimes lead to important and useful discoveries.

GEO. OLIVER.

INTRODUCTION.

THE PYTHAGOREAN TRIANGLE EXPLAINED, WITH DISSERTATION ON THE PECULIARITIES OF MASONIC NUMBER.

THE PYTHAGOREAN TRIANGLE.

INTRODUCTION.

I HAVE often wondered how it could happen that our ancient brethren should have omitted to work out the details of Freemasonry in a more particular and perfect manner than we find accomplished in the publications of the last century; because it was generally believed, even then, that such discussions would be extremely advantageous, by dissipating the mists and prejudices which biassed the minds of men, and indisposed them for the reception of truth. Numerous evidences of this fact are scattered over the writings of the few masonic authors which distinguished that period. "The best way," says Lawrie in his preface, "of refuting the calumnies which have been brought against the fraternity of Freemasons, is to lay before the public a correct and rational account of the nature, origin, and progress of the institution, that they may be enabled to determine whether or not its principles are in any shape connected with the principles of revolutionary anarchy, and whether or not the conduct of its members has ever been similar to the conduct of traitors." And from the publication of such sentiments, it must be evident to every brother's experience, that the feeling against Freemasonry, which displayed itself so openly, only a few years ago, has assumed a much milder form, if it be not entirely removed.

It will not however be difficult to account for the dearth of masonic writers in a preceding age. Before the eighteenth century, symbolical masonry, being limited to the simple ceremonial, needed few illustrations; because, as the science was chiefly operative, the most valuable secrets would be those which had a reference to building—to the scientific ornaments and decorations of each particular style of architecture as it flourished in its own exclusive period; and these mysteries were communicated gradually, as the candidate rose through the different stages of his order or profession.

There appears to have been one general principle, which extended itself over every style from the early English to the florid, decorated, and perpendicular, and constituted one of the most ineffable secrets of the Masonic Lodges. It is now known to have been the hieroglyphical device styled VESICA PISCIS; "which may be traced from the Church of St John Lateran, and the old St Peter's at Rome, to the Abbey Church at Bath, which is one of the latest Gothic buildings of any consequence in England. It was formed by two equal circles cutting each other in the centres, and was held in high veneration, having been invariably adopted by master masons in all countries. In bas-reliefs which are seen in the most ancient churches, over doorways, it usually circumscribes the figure of our Saviour. It was indeed a principle which pervaded every building dedicated to the Christian religion, and has been exclusively attributed to the scientific acquirements of Euclid."[1]

The prevailing secrets of the Lodges in these early times, were the profound dogmata of Geometry and Arithmetic, by the use of which all their complicated designs were wrought out and perfected. These sciences are inseparable from the system ; and accordingly have been faithfully transmitted to our own times. "The secret meetings of master masons within any particular district, were confined to consultations with each other, which mainly tended to the communication of science, and of improvement in their art. An evident result was seen in the general uniformity of their designs in architecture, with respect both to plan and ornament, yet not without deviations. We may conclude that the craft or mystery of architects and operative masons was involved in secrecy, by which a

[1] Kerrich in Archæol., vol. xvi. p. 292.

knowledge of their practice was carefully excluded from the acquirement of all who were not enrolled in their fraternity. Still, it was absolutely necessary that when they engaged in contracts with bishops or patrons of ecclesiastical buildings, a specification should be made of the component parts, and of the terms by which either contracting party should be rendered conversant with them. A certain nomenclature was then divulged by the master masons for such a purpose, and became in general acceptation in the middle ages."[1]

The abstruse calculations which accompanied the sciences of geometry and arithmetic, are no longer necessary to Freemasonry as an institution purely speculative; and they were accordingly omitted in the revised system as it was recommended to the notice of the fraternity by the Grand Lodge in 1717, and we retain only the beautiful theory of these sciences, with their application to the practice of morality, founded on the power and goodness of T.G.A.O.T.U.

It would be an injustice to our brethren of the last century to believe that they did not entertain a profound veneration for the principles of the masonic order. But the customs and habits of the people of England, living in that day, differed materially from our own. They were times when conviviality and a love of social harmony prevailed over the more sedate pursuits and investigations of science, in which such an

[1] Dallaway, Archit., p. 410.

astonishing progress distinguishes the present times. In the seventeenth and eighteenth centuries, London was an atmosphere of clubs, and a society of this kind existed in every street for the peculiar use of its inhabitants, besides those which were exclusively frequented by persons possessing similar tastes or habits of amusement. And it will be no disparagement to masonry, if we believe that its private Lodges did not sustain a much higher rank than some of these celebrated meetings; for the Kit-Cat, the Beefsteak, and other clubs, were frequented by the nobility and most celebrated literary characters of that polished era.

It was the organisation of Freemasonry that gave it the distinctive character which elevated its pretensions above the common routine of club-life; and although it is admitted that the members of the latter entertained a strong attachment to their several institutions, yet none were so enthusiastic as those who had enlisted in the cause of masonry, as we may learn from the few testimonies which remain. A mason of high standing, more than a century ago, thus expresses his feelings respecting the order · " Masonry is the daughter of heaven; and happy are those who embrace her. By it youth is passed over without agitation, the middle age without anxiety, and old age without remorse. Masonry teaches the way to content, a thing almost unknown to the greater part of mankind. In short, its ultimate resort is to enjoy in security the things that are, to reject all meddlers in state affairs or religion, or of a trifling nature; to embrace those of real moment and worthy tendency, with fervency and zeal unfeigned, as sure of being unchangeable as ending in happiness. They are rich without riches, intrinsically possessing all desirable good; and have the less to wish for by the enjoyment of what they have. Liberty, peace, and tranquillity, are the only objects worthy of their diligence and trouble."[1]

But this, as well as almost all the testimonies of that period to its superior excellence, is confined exclusively to the practice and rewards of Christian morality.

Modern revision has however extended the limits of scientific investigation in the order of Freemasonry beyond what was intended by those who decreed that "the privileges of masonry should no longer be restricted to operative masons, but extend to men of various professions, provided they were regularly approved and initiated into the order." And Dr Hemming and his associates, in the year 1814, thought it expedient to introduce some peculiar disquisitions from the system of Pythagoras, on the combinations of the point, the line, the superfice, and the solid, to form rectangular, trilateral, quadrilateral, multilateral figures, and the regular bodies; the latter of which, on account of their singularity, and the mysterious nature usually ascribed to them, were formerly known by the name of the

[1] Pocket Companion, p. 296.

five Platonic bodies; and they were so highly regarded by the ancient Geometricians, that Euclid is said to have composed his celebrated work on the Elements, chiefly for the purpose of displaying some of their most remarkable properties These disquisitions usually conclude with an explanation of the forty-seventh problem of Euclid, which is called the Eureka of Pythagoras.

Our transatlantic brethren have improved upon this still further. Some of their Grand Lodges have given a public sanction to the introduction of literary and scientific subjects, not contained in the usual lectures, and the open discussion of them at the private meetings of the society. And a committee of the Grand Lodge of New York, in their report for the year 1842, decided that "*masonic periodicals, if judiciously conducted, are calculated to accomplish a vast amount of good, by diffusing more extensively those sound, moral, and benevolent principles, which so eminently characterise this venerable institution;* your committee therefore recommend those publications to the liberal patronage of the fraternity."

To promote this laudable purpose, the Grand Lodges have recommended temperance and early hours; a general observance of which, I am persuaded, would not only afford ample leisure for scientific investigations, but would also operate very favourably both for the welfare and credit of the society; and it is much to be wished that such a system of discipline could be established by a similar authority in the English Lodges; for a laxity of practice in these particulars is calculated to introduce loose and incorrect habits which cannot fail to prove injurious to their popularity. If a Lodge be opened beyond the prescribed time, its labours may be protracted, particularly if it's members are too much attached to refreshment, to a late hour, which will be inconsistent with domestic comfort, and may probably create dissatisfaction and hostility in their families. There is a delicate sensibility in the female mind which is easily excited, and an impression may be made in a moment which will be found difficult to eradicate. The members of a Lodge, therefore, ought to be ever on their guard lest an unfavourable prejudice against the craft be thus created; because, in such a case, every little deviation, which, under extraordinary circumstances, may be unavoidable, will be magnified into a serious fault. And when transgressions, even though they be imaginary, are multiplied in the opinions of those who ought to be most dear to the fraternity, and whose happiness it is their duty to promote by every attention in their power, an estrangement of heart may be occasioned, which will embitter domestic comfort, and produce misunderstandings and disagreements, for which the pleasures and enjoyments of Freemasonry will be in vain expected to compensate.

Nothing can supply the loss of domestic comfort, which is the one great source of happiness that an all-wise Creator has provided for us on earth. If therefore a fear of injuring the interests of Freemasonry should fail to induce the observance of decorous hours in the conduct of a Lodge, let this consideration be superadded—let an attention to the comforts, and a respect for the prejudices of their families prompt the fraternity to avoid late sittings. It is a practice which answers no one good purpose, secures no valuable end, conveys no true gratification in the enjoyment, and embitters the reflections of the ensuing day. And beyond all this, it places in jeopardy those fireside comforts, those domestic virtues, which the religion we profess, the masonry we practise, and the reason with which the Most High has endowed us, alike concur in stimulating us to cultivate and adorn.

To carry out all these points, and to bear harmless the order during the process, much depends on the knowledge and judgment of the Master; and it is of such importance to the prosperity of Freemasonry that this officer be judiciously selected, that it behoves every candidate to consider well his capabilities for the office before his election. It is not enough that he is *au fait* at the openings and closings of the several degrees, and well acquainted with all other routine ceremonies; he ought also to be conversant with the history, the antiquities, and the philosophy of the order, and the tendency of its mysteries and pursuits to promote the practice of Christian morality; for on this knowledge the success of his administration will, in a great measure, depend. In these days, bodies of men meet together for other purposes than to hear the repeated recitation of a series of commonplace maxims, which soon lose their interest and become as sounding brass and a tinkling cymbal. Even an acquaintance with the traditions of Freemasonry is not without its utility. They lead to something of a higher character, and are intimately connected with its philosophy. The most minute legend, although abstractedly it may be considered trifling and unmeaning, is not without its use, and if traced to its elements, will be found to bear a relation to facts or doctrines connected with our best and dearest interests.

It appears to me, that in the revision of the English Ritual at the Union, a great omission occurs which it would be well to supply; and in the present taste for scientific lectures and investigations, nothing would tend to elevate the character of Freemasonry more than to afford an opportunity for its indulgence by furnishing the means of carrying out its references in the introduction of a higher range of science. Freemasonry, to be completely successful, should take precedence in science as it does in morals and the exercise of charity: for there are few institutions which equal it in the walks of benevolence. Its charities are unrivalled. It cherishes the orphan —it supports the widow—it relieves the destitute —and provides for the worthy aged brother an asylum from the storms of penury and indigence, at that helpless period of life when his strength fails him, and he is no longer able to wrestle successfully with adversity and want.

It is true the seven liberal sciences are referred to in the second degree ; but, with the exception of Geometry, they occupy no important place in the lecture. And for this reason, I suppose, that in ancient times the order was denominated Geometry. On this science, with its application to architecture, our disquisitions are abundant and powerfully interesting ; and why should not a lecture on the elementary principles of other sciences be equally gratifying to the members of a Lodge ? Arithmetic, or the science of Number, is nearly allied to Geometry ; we patronise Music in practice but hear nothing of it in theory; and of Astronomy we are merely told that it is an art by which we are taught to read the wonderful works of God in those sacred pages the celestial hemisphere, and that while we are employed in the study of this science, we perceive unparalleled instances of wisdom and goodness, and through the whole of the creation trace the glorious Author by His works.

That great philosopher Pythagoras, who, by the superiority of his mind, infused a new spirit into the science and learning of Greece, and founded the Italic sect, taught his disciples Geometry, that they might be able to deduce a reason for all their thoughts and actions, and to ascertain correctly the truth or falsehood of any proposition by the unerring process of mathematical demonstration. Thus being enabled to contemplate the reality of things, and to detect imposture and deceit, they were pronounced to be on the road to perfect happiness. Such was the discipline and teaching of the Pythagorean Lodges. It is related, that when Justin Martyr applied to a learned Pythagorean to be admitted as a candidate for the mysterious dogmata of his philosophy, he was asked whether, as a preliminary step, he had already studied the sciences of Arithmetic, Music, Astronomy, and Geometry, which were esteemed the four divisions of the mathematics; and he was told that it was impossible to understand the perfection of beatitude without them, because they alone are able to abstract the soul from sensibles, and to prepare it for intelligibles. He was further told that in the absence of these sciences no man is able to contemplate what is honest, or to determine what is good. And because the candidate acknowledged his ignorance of them he was refused admission into the society.

Above all other sciences or parts of the mathematics, however, the followers of Pythagoras esteemed the doctrine of NUMBERS, which they believed to have been revealed to man by the celestial deities. And they pronounced Arithmetic to be the most ancient of all the sciences, because, being naturally first generated, it takes away the rest with itself, but is not taken away with them. For instance, animal is first in nature before man; for by taking away animal we take away man; but by taking away man we do not take away animal. They considered numbers extending to the decad, to be the cause of the essence of all other things; and therefore esteemed the creation of the world as nothing more than the harmonious effect of a pure arrangement of number. This idea has been adopted by Dryden—

> From harmony, from heavenly harmony,
> This universal frame began;
> From harmony to harmony,
> Through all the compass of the notes it ran,
> The diapason closing full in man.

Pythagoras had another idea, as we are informed by Censorinus, respecting the creation of the world, and taught that it was fashioned according to the principles of musical proportion; that the seven planets which govern the nativity of mortals have a harmonious motion, and intervals corresponding to musical diastemes, and render various sounds according to their several distances, so perfectly consonant that they make the sweetest melody, but "inaudible to us by reason of the greatness of the noise, which the narrow passage of our ears is incapable of receiving."

And further, he esteemed the monad to represent the great and good Creator, under the name of *Dis*, or *Zeus*, or *Zau;* and the duad he referred to the evil and counteracting principle or dæmon, "surrounded," as Plutarch expresses it,[1] "with a mass of matter." And Porphyry adds,[2] that the monad and duad of Pythagoras seem to have been the same with Plato's πέρας and ἄπειρον, his *finite* and *infinite* in his Philebus; the former

[1] De Placitis Placitorum, l. i. c. 7.   [2] Vit. Pyth., p. 47.

of which two only is substantial, that first most simple Being, the cause of all unity and the measure of all things.

According to the above doctrine, the monad was esteemed the father of Number, and the duad its mother : whence the universal prejudice in favour of odd numbers, the father being had in greater honour than the mother. Odd numbers being masculine were considered perfect, and applicable to the celestial gods, while even numbers, being female, were considered imperfect, and given to the terrestrial and infernal deities. Virgil has recorded several instances of this predilection in favour of odd numbers. In his eighth Eclogue, he says,

> Terna tibi hæc primum triplici diversa colore
> Licia circumdo; terque hæc altaria circum
> Effigiem duco; *Numero deos impare gaudet.*

Thus translated by Dryden—

> Around his waxen image first I wind
> Three woollen fillets of three colours join'd ;
> Thrice bind about his thrice-devoted head,
> Which round the sacred altar thrice is led.
> *Unequal numbers please the gods.*

The Eastern nations of the present day appear to reverse this principle. When two young persons are betrothed, the number of letters in each of their names is subtracted the one from the other, and if the remainder be an even number, it is considered a favourable omen, but if it be odd, the inference is that the marriage will be unfortunate.

Some curious superstitions of this character were still in existence during the last century amongst ourselves, and may not at the present time be altogether obsolete. A Scottish minister, who wrote a treatise on witchcraft in 1705, says, "Are there not some who cure diseases by the charm of numbers, after the example of Balaam, who used *magiam geometricam,* Build me here seven altars, and prepare me seven oxen and seven rams. There are some witches who enjoin the sick to dip their shirts seven times in water that runs towards the south." Sir Henry Ellis has collected many instances of the use of odd numbers, in his notes on Brand's "Popular Antiquities," to which the curious reader is referred.[1]

The superstition of divination by number, called Arithomancy, was so firmly planted in the mind of man by the observances of ancient times, that it appears impossible entirely to eradicate it. An old writer quaintly remarks, "I will not be superstitiously opinionated of the misteries of numbers, though it bee of longe standing amongst many learned men; neither will I positively affirm that the number of six is fatall to weomen, and the numbers of seaven and nine to men; or that those numbers have (as many have written) *magnum in tota rerum natura potestatem,* great power in kingdoms and commonwealths, in families, ages, of bodies, sickness, health, wealth, losse, &c. ; or

[1] See also on this subject Censor. de die nat., e. xii. Philo de leg., i. Bodin de Repub., l. iv. c. 2. Varro in Gell., l. iii. Jerom in Amos, v. Practice of Piety, fol. 410, &c. &c.

with Seneca and others, *Septimus quisque annus,* &c. Each seaventh yeare is remarkable with men, as the sixth is with weomen. Or, as divines teach, that in the number of seaven there is a misticall perfection which our understandinge cannot attaine unto; and that nature herself is observant of this number."

Every tyro knows that odd numbers are masonic; and if he be ignorant of the reasons why 3, 5, 7, and 11, have been adopted as landmarks, let him apply to the Master of his Lodge for information, and he will then be satisfied of the wisdom of the appropriation, because number forms one of the pillars which contribute to the support of scientific masonry, and constitutes an elementary principle of Geometry. Thus, in the celebrated Pythagorean triangle, consisting of ten points, the upper single dot or jod is monad or unity, and represents a *point,* for Pythagoras considered a point to correspond in proportion to unity; a *line* to 2; a *superfice* to 3; a *solid* to 4; and he defined a point as a monad having position, and the beginning of all things; a line was thought to correspond with duality, because it was produced by the first motion from indivisible nature, and formed the junction of two points. A superfice was compared to the number three, because it is the first of all causes that are found in figures; for a circle, which is the principal of all round figures, comprises a triad, in centre—space—circumference. But a triangle, which is the first of all rectilineal figures, is included in a ternary, and receives its form according to that number; and was considered by the Pythagoreans to be the author of all sublunary things. The four points at the base of the Pythagorean triangle correspond with a solid or cube, which combines the principles of length, breadth, and thickness, for no solid can have less than four extreme boundary points.

Thus it appears that in applying number to physical things, the system of Pythagoras terminated in a tetrad, while that of Aristotle, by omitting the point, limited the doctrine of magnitude to a triad, viz., line—surface—body. In divine things, however, the former philosopher profusely used the number three, because it represented the three principal attributes of the Deity. The first whereof, as we are informed by Cudworth, is infinite with fecundity; the second infinite knowledge and wisdom; and the last active and perceptive power. From which divine attributes the Pythagoreans and Platonists seem to have framed their trinity of archical hypostases, such as have the nature of principles in the universe, and which, though they be apprehended as several distinct substances gradually subordinate to one another, yet they many times extend the τὸ Θεῖον so far as to comprehend them all within it.

While employed in investigating the curious and unique properties which distinguish many of the digits, we no longer wonder that the inhabitants of the ancient world, in their ignorance of the mysterious secrets of science, and the abstruse doctrine of causes and effects, should have ascribed to the immediate interposition of the Deity those miraculous results which may be produced by an artful combination of particular numbers. Even philosophy was staggered; and the most refined theorists entertained singular fancies, which they were unable to solve without having recourse to supernatural agency. Hence the pseudo science of Arithomancy, or divination by numbers, became very prevalent in the ancient world; and was used by Pythagoras as an actual emanation of the Deity. By this means, according to Tzetzes, he not only was able to foretel future events, but reduced the doctrine to a science, governed by specific rules, which he transmitted to posterity in his "Book of Prognostics."

The ancients had a kind of onomantic arithmetic, the invention of which was in like manner ascribed to Pythagoras, whether truly or not is of no importance here, in which the letters of the alphabet, the planets, the days of the week, and the twelve zodiacal signs, were assimilated with certain numbers; and thus, by the use of prescribed tables, constructed astrologically according to the aspects, qualities, dignities, and debilities of the planets relatively towards the twelve signs, &c., the adept would authoritatively pronounce an opinion on questions affecting life and death, good and evil fortune, journeys, detection of theft, or the success of an enterprise. It must be confessed, however, that these predictions were not always correct; for the rules laid down in different systems varied so essentially, that the wisest magician was frequently puzzled to select an appropriate interpretation. The numeral system has been introduced into the modern practice of astrology, and very important results appear to depend on the trine, quartile, and sextile aspect of the planets in the horoscope.

Something of this sort was used by the Jewish cabalists; and hence one of the rules of their cabala was called *gemetria*, or numeration, which was chiefly confined to the interpretation of their sacred writings. The letters of the Hebrew language being numerals, and the whole Bible being composed of different combinations of those letters, it was supposed that the correct meaning of difficult passages could only be ascertained by resorting to their numerical value. The Talmudists entertained an opinion that the mystery of numbers was actually taught in their scriptures; because, after the idolatrous priests of Baal had accepted the challenge of Elijah, that prophet constructed his altar of twelve stones, corresponding with the twelve tribes of Israel; but they say that when he took this number for the special purpose of conciliating the favour of Jehovah, it was not merely because the sons of Jacob were twelve in number, but because that particular number was supposed to contain a profound and unfathomable mystery.

The system on which this doctrine was founded appears to be, that every letter in the Hebrew alphabet is in reality a distinct light or attribute; and hence the letters are symbols of everything which the earth and heavens contain. The Rabbi Baraliel taught that numbers proceed from Him who was before all numbers, as they go not beyond ten. These lights are denominated ספירה in the singular, which is derived from ספר numbers; each possessing the property of the number which it represents. And hence the theologians say that the Tetragrammaton represents the Ten Sovereign Lights, in which all the divinity is infused, because the words formed by these letters are invariable; and although they admit of twelve transpositions and combinations, every one of them means T.G.A.O.T.U. Hence the prophet Malachi says, "I am the Lord, and change not;" for the Tetragrammaton, or Sacred Name, however it may be transposed, never changes its meaning.

The Rabbi Manasseh, Ben Israel, in his explanation of the cabala, says, "The fourth rule is founded on the shape of the letters. If it be asked, Why does the law begin with a ב ? The answer is, Because it is formed by three lines, or ו's, which, being written at length, spell ואו, numerically thirteen; this number being multiplied by three (the three lines), makes thirty-nine, equal to ידוה אהד (the Lord is One), also thirty-nine. The cabalists say that this letter ב has a point above and another behind, signifying that the Lord who is in heaven created the world, which is represented by the antecedent letter, that is the א, formed by two י's and a ו, making together twenty-six, the same number as the Tetragrammaton. Reason apparently supports the idea that profound mysteries are contained in the characters of this holy language; and who will contend that they do not all involve many secrets and reasons for being used in the law of God, from the perfect art with which they are formed?"

The same results were obtained by means of the Magic Square, which is a figure made up of numbers in arithmetical proportion, so disposed in parallel and equal ranks that the sums of each row, whether taken perpendicularly, horizontally, or diagonally, are equal, as in the adjoining diagram. Such squares seem to have been so called because they were used in the construction of talismans. It is probable they were so employed in

2	7	6
9	5	1
4	3	8

consequence of the ranks always making the same sum, a circumstance extremely surprising in the more ignorant ages, when mathematics passed for magic. The magic square was held in great veneration among the Egyptians; and the Pythagoreans, their disciples, in order to add more efficacy and virtue to this square, dedicated it to the then known seven planets divers ways, and engraved it upon a plate of that particular metal which was esteemed in sympathy with the planet.

The square thus dedicated was enclosed within a regular polygon inscribed in a circle, which was divided into as many equal parts as there were units in the side of the square, with the names of the angles of the planet; and the signs of the zodiac written upon the void spaces between the polygon and the circumference of the circumscribing circle. Such a talisman they vainly imagined would befriend the person who carried it about with him.[1]

Divination by numbers was not confined to Jewish or heathen nations, but occupied much attention at different periods of Christianity; and superstitious properties, I am afraid, are still attached to particular numbers, as forming climacterics, or grand climacterics; for the days of a man's life are usually considered to be affected by the septenary year, which, as it is frequently believed, produces considerable changes in both body and mind. But the most remarkable change in a person's life is at the climacteric, or $7 \times 7 = 49$ years; or the grand climacteric, $7 \times 9 = 63$; or $9 \times 9 = 81$ years; each of which is conceived to be fraught with a peculiar fatality. And there are numbers of persons, even in the nineteenth century, who contemplate these periods with some degree of terror, and esteem it a relief when they have passed away.

Several other numbers have superstitious meanings attached to them. Dr Brown, in his

[1] See more of this in Chambers's Tracts, under the head of "Natural Magic."

"Pseudodoxia Epidemica," says that "six have found many leaves in its favour; not only for the daies of the creation, but its natural consideration as being a perfect number, and the first that is completed by its parts; that is, the sixt, the half, and the third, 1, 2, 3; which drawn into a sum, makes six. The number ten hath been as highly extolled, as containing even, odd, long, plane, quadrate, and cubical numbers; and Aristotle observed with admiration that barbarians as well as Greeks did use a numeration unto ten; which, being so general, was not to be judged casual, but to have a foundation in nature. So not only seven and nine, but all the rest have had their elogies, as may be observed at large in Rhodiginus, and in several writers; since every one extolling number according to his subject, and as it advantaged the present discourse in hand."

On the same subject, Smith, in his "Life of William, Marquis of Berkeley," who was born in 1426, tells us that he "closeth the second septenary number from Harding the Dane, as much differing from his last ancestors, as the Lord Thomas, the first septenary lord, did from his six former forefathers." And he then proceeds to say, "I will not be superstitiously opinionated of the misteries of numbers, though it bee of longe standing amongst many learned men; neither will I positively affirm that the number of six is fatall to weomen, and the numbers of seaven and nine to men; or that those numbers have (as many have written) *magnum in tota rerum natura potestatem,* great power in kingdoms and commonwealths, in families, ages, of bodies, sickness, health, wealth, losse, &c.; or with Seneca and others, *Septimus quisque annus,* &c. Each seaventh yeare is remarkable with men, as the sixth is with weomen. Or, as divines teach, that in the number of seaven there is a misticall perfection which our understandinge cannot attaine unto; and that nature herself is observant of this number."

Numeral divination on some unimportant points was at length reduced to an unerring system; and the memory of a few brief rules would enable even a child to dive into another's thoughts, and thus excite a high degree of astonishment, by a process which cannot fail to produce a correct result. For instance, if any person has an *even* number of counters in one hand, and an *odd* number in the other, it will be easy to determine in which hand the odd or even number is by the following certain rule. Desire the person to multiply the number in his right hand by any odd figure, and the number in his left by an even one; and inform you whether the products when added together are odd or even. If even, the even number is in the right hand; if odd, the even number is in the left hand.

By a similar process, a number which any person may think of will be easily ascertained. Thus, request him to double the number with the addition of four; then let him multiply the whole by five, adding twelve to the product, and placing a cipher after the amount. From the number thus obtained let him deduct 320 and tell you the remainder; from which, if you reject the two last figures, the number that remains will be the one which he had fixed on in his mind. I shall close these observations on the subject of numeral divination with one other example. If you would find the difference between two numbers, the greatest of which is unknown, it will only be necessary to take as many nines as there are figures in the smallest number, and subtract that sum from the number of nines. Let another add that difference to the largest number, and taking away the first figure of the amount, add it to the number that remains, and that sum will be the difference required.

In these times of superior scientific knowledge, when gas has superseded the use of oil, and steam performs the labour of men and horses; when sage philosophers have discovered mushrooms in potatoes, and sledge-hammers in the pollen of wheat, these topics may be considered puerile and useless; but it was not so at that period— of ignorance, as it may be esteemed by modern presumption—when the standard of learning and wit was borne by such men as Addison and Steele, Pope, Swift, Johnson, and their coadjutors, the jewels of the Augustan crown, when such subjects were esteemed worthy the notice of a *Spectator*, a *Rambler*, a *Guardian*, or a *World*.

Dr Johnson, speaking in the *Rambler* of the

climacteric periods, says, "The writers of medicine and physiology have traced, with great appearance of accuracy, the effects of time upon the human body, by marking the various periods of the constitution and the several stages by which animal life makes its progress from infancy to decrepitude. Though their observations have not enabled them to discover how manhood may be accelerated, or old age retarded, yet surely, if they be considered only as the amusements of curiosity, they are of equal importance with conjectures on those things more remote, with catalogues of the fixed stars and calculations of the bulk of planets. It had been a task worthy of the greatest philosophers to have considered with equal care the climacterics of the mind; to have pointed out the time at which every passion begins and ceases to predominate, and noted the regular variations of desire, and the succession of one appetite to another."

Amongst the ancients, number was divided into two distinct parts, intellectual and sciential. The former was considered the root and origin of all things; the cause of the existence of gods and men; the principle of the universe and all that it contains, by which matter was arranged into form and order, and the systems perform their accustomed revolutions with accuracy and precision. The sciential division was subdivided into two portions, odd and even, the former limited, the latter infinite. According to the definition used by the Pythagoreans, "even number is that which at once admits division into the greatest and the least; into the greatest magnitudes (for halves are the greatest parts); the least in multitude (for two is the least number) according to the natural opposition of these two kinds. Odd numbers cannot be thus divided; for they are only capable of being separated into two unequal parts." Pythagoras called the monad the father, and the duad the mother of number; whence it was concluded that those numbers which resembled the monad were most propitious.

Hence, in all the heathen systems, odd numbers were esteemed the most perfect, and represented the celestial deities. In our own country however, and under the influence of Christianity, we find a predilection for even numbers in connection with the mysteries of fairy mythology so prevalent in the middle ages. In Morgan's "Phœnix Brittanicus" is a curious tract on this subject, entitled "An account of Anne Jefferis, now living in the county of Cornwall, who was fed for six months by a small sort of airy people called fairies; and of the strange and wonderful cures she performed with salves and medicines she received from them, for which she never took one penny of her patients" In this tract she gives the following account of her commerce with these creatures, which I quote so far as it applies to my purpose. She says, "that in 1645, as she was one day sitting knitting in an arbour in the garden, there came over the hedge, of a sudden, *six* persons of a small stature, all clothed in green, which frighted her so much as to throw her into a great sickness. They continued their appearance to her never less than two at a time, and never more than eight, *and always in even numbers*, 2, 4, 6, 8."

In order to a right understanding of the application of the numeral system, it will be necessary to give a detailed explanation of the occult meaning of the several digits, as taught in some of the ancient systems of the spurious Freemasonry; and this will show to what a beautiful moral purpose it is capable of being applied.

THE MONAD, OR POINT, DISCUSSED AS THE ORIGIN OF ALL CALCULATION.

THE POINT, MONAD, UNITY, OR THE NUMBER ONE.

CHAPTER I.

THE POINT.

MONAD, UNITY, OR THE NUMBER ONE.

"A POINT is enough to put all the schools in the world in a combustion. But what need has man to know that point, since the creation of such a small being is beyond his power? *A fortiori*, philosophy acts against probability when, from that point which absorbs and disconcerts all her meditations, she presumes to pass on to the generation of the world, or the ordering of God's decrees."
—LA PLUCHE.

>"The sciences may well compose
> A noble structure, vast;
> A point, a line, a superfice,
> But solid is the last."
> ANCIENT LECTURES OF MASONRY.

THE exalted ideas which were entertained by the ancient poets and philosophers respecting the mysterious properties of numbers, may be estimated from the superstitious uses to which they were made subservient in all countries, whether the inhabitants were savage or refined. The former saw that the number of his fingers ended at ten; and this constituted the amount of his knowledge. It formed the standard of all his computations. When a savage, on his war-path, was asked the number of his enemies—if few, he would hold up one or more of his fingers—if many, them all. And in whatever manner his ideas of units might be designated, the calculation would always end in ten. Thus, in Homer, Proteus counts his sea-calves by fives, or in other words by the number of fingers on his hand. Several nations in the wilds of America have to this day no other instruments of calculation. It is another strong presumption of the truth of what I now advance, that all civilised nations count by tens; tens of tens, or hundreds; tens of hundreds, or thousands; and so on, but always from ten to ten. We can discover no reason why this number should be chosen rather than any other for the term of numeration, except the primitive practice of counting by the fingers.[1]

This was the general custom, although there were some exceptions. For instance, M. de la Condamine tells us of a certain tribe in South America who had no particular word for any number beyond three;[2] while in Mexico and Central America they added this three to their ten fingers, and counted as far as thirteen; beyond which point they again commenced with the unit. But the rule will hold good for the general usage of antiquity; and as such has been delivered down to our own times.

[1] Goguet, Origin of Laws, vol. i. p. 216.
[2] Relat. de la rivière des Amazones, p. 67.

Arithmetical operations, says the Abbé Pluche,[1] were facilitated and shortened first by the use of counters, and afterwards by figures or chalked letters. Thus the Romans, when they had a mind to express unity, either held up one finger or chalked the figure I. To express the succeeding numbers they drew II, III, IIII. For the number five they depressed the three middle fingers, and extended the thumb and little finger only, which formed the V. They signified ten by putting two V's, one upon the other, thus $_\Lambda^V$, or by joining them together, which formed X. Then they combined the X, the V, and the I, till they came up to fifty, or five tens, which they expressed by laying the five upon its side, thus, ∠. The figure in this posture assumed the form of an L. A hundred was marked with two L's put one upon the other ($_L^\Gamma$), which was subsequently rounded into a C. Five hundred was expressed by Lↄ, and a thousand by CLↄ. These figures were afterwards changed, the one into D, and the other into CIↄ, or M. The Greeks and Hebrews employed the letters of the alphabet ranged in order, to express all imaginable numbers.

It was the belief of wise and learned men in all ages that there was a secret virtue in particular numbers, amongst whom Pythagoras occupies the principal rank. He was followed by all the philosophers of the Italic school; and Plato transmitted it, with many improvements, to his suc-

[1] Spectacle de la Nature, vol. v. p. 141.

cessors; until the superstition became so firmly grafted in the human mind, that time and education have failed entirely to extinguish it. An examination into the mysterious properties of numbers has constituted the serious occupation of many a man of real talent in comparatively modern times. But the old philosophers embodied in their numeral system such excellent doctrines, and beautiful lessons of morality as have been deemed worthy of introduction into the science of Freemasonry for the edification of the brethren; and the absurd superstitions in which they were originally embodied may be forgiven, as being incidental to their imperfect and spurious religion, for the sake of the genius with which they were decorated and enriched.

Amongst these sages, the MONAD represented the throne of the Omnipotent Deity, placed in the centre of the empyrean, to indicate T.G.A.O.T.U., by whom all things were made and are preserved. This disposition was symbolised by the hierogram of a Point within a circle or equilateral triangle, to exemplify equally the unity of the divine essence, and His eternity, having neither beginning of years nor end of days. And this deduction appears perfectly reasonable, because the Monad or Point is the original and cause of the entire numeral system, as God is the cause of all things, being the only and great Creator on whom everything depends; for, if there were more all-powerful Beings than one, none would be independent, nor would all perfections be centred in one individual, "neither formally by reason of their distinction, nor eminently and virtually, for then one should have power to produce the other, and that nature which is producible is not divine. But all acknowledge God to be absolutely and infinitely perfect, in whom all perfections imaginable, which are simply such, must be contained formally, and all others which imply any mixture of perfection, virtually."[1]

And to the same effect, Sthenidas the Locrian says, "The first god is conceived to be the father both of gods and men, because he is mild to everything which is in subjection to him, and never ceases to govern with providential regard. Nor is he alone satisfied with being the maker of all things, but he is the nourisher, the preceptor of everything beautiful, and the legislator to all things equally."[2]

The universal symbol by which this great Being was designated, viz., *the point within a circle*, it may be necessary to explain with some degree of minuteness, because it constitutes one of the most important emblems of masonry. One of the earliest heathen philosophers of whom history gives any account was Hermes Trismegistus, and he describes the Maker of the universe as "an intelligible sphere whose centre is everywhere, and whose circumference cannot be defined," because the universe is boundless, and He existed

---

[1] Pearson on the Creed, Art. 1.
[2] Taylor's Fragments, p. 27.

from all eternity. David expressed a similar sentiment when he said, "Thou art the same, and Thy years will have no end."[1] We are told that the Persians, when they wished to pay a high respect to the Deity, ascended to the top of a high mountain, and expanding both hands, they prayed to Him in the name of "the circle of heaven." In like manner, the Jews entertained a belief that "the heaven of heavens could not contain Him." The Romans placed a circular target as a symbol of the Deity, because, as in the circumference there is but one point at its centre, and can be no more, so in the whole circumference of the universe there can be only one perfect and powerful God; nor is it possible there should be another.

I have received a suggestion from a very intelligent brother respecting this symbol, which merits consideration. He says, When the W.M. elect enters into the obligation of an Installed Master, the brethren form a circle round him, he being in the centre; and in this situation he is said to be the representative of Solomon, the son of David. Now, as this is unquestionably a Christian degree, I understand this son of David to be a figurative expression for the Redeemer of mankind. The W.M. is then specially intrusted with the Holy Scriptures, and invested with a jewel which is emblematical thereof, and it then becomes his duty to exhort his brethren to search those Scriptures, because they contain the words

[1] Psalm cii. 28.

of eternal life, and testify to the divinity of Christ. Searching implies something lost; and our ancient brethren, the early Christians, after they had lost, by an untimely death, their Lord and Master, remembered that while assembled together in Lodge here below, He had promised that when two or three were gathered together in His name, He would be *in the midst of them;* and cheered by the recollection, they were naturally led to hope that He would always be found in the centre of their circle, whenever regularly assembled together in a just and perfect Lodge dedicated to God and holy St John. In like manner, we are reminded by that sacred symbol that He is always in the midst of us—that His all-seeing eye is always upon us, and therefore exhorted to discharge our duty towards Him and our fellow-creatures with freedom, fervency, and zeal.

The Monad, amongst the Grecian philosophers, was a symbol of the hermaphrodite deity, or junction of the sexes, because it partakes of two natures.[1] In a mysterious passage of the Yajur Veda, Brahma is spoken of, after his emanation from the golden egg, as experiencing fear at being alone in the universe; he therefore willed the existence of another, and instantly became masculo-feminine. The two sexes thus existing in one god were immediately, by another act of volition, divided in twain, and became man and wife. This tradition seems to have found its way into

---

[1] Macrob. in somn. Scip., i. 6.

Greece; for the Androgyne of Plato is but another version of this Oriental myth.[1] If the Monad be added to an odd number, it makes it even, and if to an even number, it makes it odd. Hence it was called Jupiter, because it stands at the head of numbers, as Jupiter is at the head of gods and men; and also Vesta or Fire, because, like the point within a circle, it is seated in the midst of the world. It was also called the Throne of Jupiter, from the great power which the centre has in the universe, being able to restrain its general circular motion, as if the custody of the Maker of all things were constituted therein.[2]

Plutarch tells us that Numa built a temple in an orbicular form for the preservation of the sacred fire; intending by the fashion of the edifice to shadow out, not so much the earth as the whole universe; in the centre of which the Pythagoreans placed Fire, which they called Vesta and *Unity*. The Persians worshipped the *circumference*, but it could only refer to the apparent course of the sun in the firmament, which is the boundary of common observation; for the real circumference is far beyond the comprehension of finite man. And the sun, under the symbol of a point within a circle, was the great object of worship amongst the Dionysian artists who built the Temple of Solomon.

On this interesting subject a learned and intelligent brother offers the following opinion in a

[1] The Hindoos, vol. i. p. 166.
[2] Procl. in Timæum, com. iv.

letter to the author : The more I study the subject of masonry, the more I am convinced that the mysteries were unknown at Jerusalem till introduced by the Dionysian artificers;[1] and that the ceremonies were astronomical, mixed with paganism and sun-worship. I believe also that Solomon divested them of their evil tendency, and created a new legend ; but that the main object was an astronomical emblem. The Jews did not require masonry to keep them religious; for their religion was open to all, whereas that of the Dionysians was known only to the initiated. Masonry could not then be used for a religious purpose among the Jews, although the ceremonial may have been adapted at that time to both Jew and Gentile ; so that the Dionysian artists thenceforth transmitted the meaning of the point within a circle, not as bearing any reference to sun-worship, but as regarding the sun merely as a great work of the one uncreated God. Thus the emblems of the sun and moon became introduced into masonry; and however we may explain them in our Lodges, they appear to me unquestionable remains of the solar worship, or at least of astronomy.

For some such reason Hierocles the Pythagorean concluded that " the gods are immutable, and firm in their decrees ; so that they never change the conception of what appeared to them to be fit from the beginning. Hence they were likened

[1] See Joseph Hippolita's D'Acosta's Sketch of the Dionysian Artificers.

to the Monad; because there is one immutability and firmness of the virtues, which it is reasonable to suppose subsists transcendently with the gods, and which imparts a never-failing stability to their conceptions." Under this description the Monad represented Mind, because it is stationary;[1] and for a similar reason it was called Good;[2] and seminal power, because it is the root, origin, and summary of all numbers[3] It was also considered the vehicle of number, as a ship at sea or a chariot on land contains many persons and things; and hence it had the name of both these vessels.

It was a symbol of love and friendship; and taught the mild Pythagoreans the doctrine of forgiveness of injuries; for they argued—Will not a man who is a brother, or even any casual person, who deserves attention in a much greater degree than a brute, be changed to milder manners by proper treatment, though he should not entirely forsake his rusticity? In our behaviour, therefore, towards every man, and in a much greater degree towards a brother, we should imitate the reply of Socrates to one who said to him, "May I die unless I am revenged on you." For his answer was, "May I die if I do not make you my friend."

The Monad further signified Chaos, the father of life, substance, the cause of Truth, reason, and the receptacle of all things. Also in greater and

---

[1] Alex. Aphrod. in metaph.   [2] Porph. vit. Pyth.
[3] Mart. Capel., vii.

lesser it signified *equal;* in intention and remission, *middle;* in multitude, *mean;* in time, *now*, the present, because it consists in one part of time which is always present.[1] The cabalists considered that the first eternal principle is magical, and like a hidden fire, is eternally known in its colours, in the figure, in the wisdom of God, as in a looking-glass. The magical centre of the first principle is fire, which is as a spirit, without palpable substance.

The number one symbolised the Platonic, or rather the Pythagorean doctrine of Benevolence. Thus Hierocles[2] says, "Each of us is, as it were, circumscribed by many concentric circles; some of which are less, but others larger, and some comprehend, but others are comprehended, according to the different and unequal habitudes with respect to each other. For the first and most proximate circle is that which every one describes about his own mind *as a centre*, in which circle the body, and whatever is assumed for the sake of the body, are comprehended. For this is nearly the smallest circle, and almost touches the centre itself. The second from this, and which is at a greater distance from the centre, but comprehends the first circle, is that in which parents, brothers, wife, and children are arranged. The third circle from the centre is that which contains uncles and aunts, grandfathers and grandmothers, and the children of brothers and sisters.

[1] Macrob. in somn., l. i. s. 6.
[2] Ethical Fragments of Hierocles, by Taylor, p. 106.

After this is the circle which comprehends the remaining relatives. Next to this is that which contains the common people, then that which comprehends those of the same tribe, afterwards that which contains the citizens; and then two other circles follow, one being the circle of those that dwell in the vicinity of the city, and the other of those of the same province. But the outermost and greatest circle, and which comprehends all the other circles, is that of the whole human race." This admirable passage, says Taylor, is so conformable to the following beautiful lines in Pope's "Essay on Man," that it is most probably the source from whence they were derived—

> Self-love but serves the virtuous mind to wake,
> As the small pebble stirs the peaceful lake;
> The centre moved, a circle straight succeeds,
> Another still, and still another spreads;
> Friend, parent, neighbour, first it will embrace,
> His country next, and next all human race;
> Wide and more wide the o'erflowings of the mind,
> Take every creature in of every kind.

The learned Aben Ezra, on the 11th chapter of Daniel, says, that the number *one* is in a manner the cause of all numbers, and is besides a complete number; it causes multiplication and remainder, but does not admit of either itself. And in another place he says, "Numbers are founded on the unit one." The sage Latif observes the same. According to Euclid, in his second definition of the seventh book, numbers are formed of many units; but unity being indivisible, has no composition, nor is it a number, but the fountain and mother of all numbers. Being the cause of all numbers, they are formed by a plurality of units. Thus 2 is twice 1; 3 is three units, &c.; so that all numbers require the Monad, while it exists by itself without requiring any other. All which is to be considered of the First Cause; for as *one* is no number, but the cause and beginning of number, so the First Cause has no affinity to creatures, but is the cause and beginning of them; they all stand in need of Him, and He requires assistance from none. He is all in all, and all are included in Him in the most simple unity. The Jewish Rabbins agree that He is One, and there is no unity like His in the universe; the nearest idea that we can form of Him is symbolised by the unit or the figure ONE.[1]

The Pythagoreans say, " The Monad is the principle of all things. From the Monad came the indeterminate duad, as matters subjected to the cause, Monad; from the Monad and indeterminate duad, Numbers; from numbers, *Points;* points, *Lines;* from lines, *Superfices;* from superfices, *Solids;* from these solid Bodies, whose elements are four, Fire, Water, Air, Earth; of all which, transmutated, and totally changed, the World consists." [2]

But Freemasonry has a peculiar reference for

---

[1] Manasseh ben Israel, Concil., vol. i. p. 105.
[2] Laert. in vit. Pyth.

the Monad, which produces some very striking and remarkable coincidences in every nation under the sun. In an old ritual of the Fellow Craft's degree, used about the middle of the last century, we find the following passage in reference equally to the first step of the winding staircase, the Point, and the letter G: "God, the great Architect of the Universe, whom it is at all times our duty to worship and obey." In a ritual still more ancient, the same meaning is rather differently expressed, viz., "the Grand Architect and Contriver of the Universe; or He that was taken up to the topmost pinnacle of the Holy Temple."

This acknowledgment of the divine unity, or point within either a circle or a triangle, was common to all the systems of Spurious Freemasonry that ever existed, from India and Japan to the extremest west, including the Goths, the Celts, and the aborigines of America. All acknowledge the unity of T.G.A.O.T.U., whether involved in the deepest ignorance, or refined by civilisation and a knowledge of philosophy and science. The sages of Greece, through a series of wire-drawn reasoning, came to the same conclusion as the uninformed savages of Britain, Scandinavia, Mexico, or Peru.

It may be useful to examine a few of these systems, all emanating from the Spurious Freemasonry, to show the bearing of this universal belief, which will prove the superiority of revelation over the speculations of unassisted reason.

The Divine Being was called by the Romans Jove, or JAH; by the Chaldeans, the Phœnicians, and the Celtæ, Bel or BUL; and by the Indians and Egyptians, *Aum* (Om) or ON. The first was plainly Jehovah; the second was a common name of God; and the last was used by the early Christians to express the Being whom they worshipped. Ὁ ὪΝ, καὶ ὁ ἦν, καὶ ὁ ἐρχόμενος, God, which is, and was, and is to come.[1] But it must always be kept in mind that the heathen, in acknowledging their chief god to be the Maker or G.A.O.T.U., did not understand it in the exact sense in which it is received by Jews and Christians. They believed that God built the world *out of existing materials;* we are satisfied that He created it out of nothing. The divine unity was plainly revealed to the Jews at their deliverance from the bondage of Egypt. Thus when Moses promulgated the Law, he said, "Hear, O Israel: The Lord our God is one Lord."[2] This declaration was so frequently repeated, that the Jews, amidst all their rebellious and religious defections, never doubted its truth. In like manner, the Vedas of India, the Zends of Persia, the Hermesian writings of Egypt, the Eddas of the northern nations of Europe, &c., all contained the same truth; and from these original sources, it was conveyed through Thales and Pythagoras to the philosophers of Greece and Rome.

The latter great philosopher styled the Supreme

[1] Rev. i. 4. [2] Deut. vi. 4.

Deity το εν, the UNITY, and μονας, the MONAD; a term by which he doubtless intended to express his conception of the simplicity as well as purity of the divine nature. As the sole cause and first principle of all that exists, Pythagoras esteemed the Deity to be *the centre of unity* and source of harmony. He likewise conferred on this Almighty Sovereign the name by which Plato afterwards distinguished the first hypostasis of his triad, το αγαθον, *the chief good.* From this eternal Monad, however, from this primeval UNITY, according to Pythagoras and all his disciples, there sprang an infinite duality.[1]

The philosophers of most nations entertained similar opinions respecting the undivided unity of the Supreme God, which they learned through the medium of the Spurious Freemasonry. Zoroaster is sublime in his description of the Deity; but he had enjoyed the advantage of associating with the learned Jews at Babylon, and from them, doubtless, he had acquired his knowledge. He taught that "God is the First; incorruptible, eternal, unmade, indivisible, not like anything, the author of all good, the wisest of the wise, the father of justice, self-taught, and absolutely perfect."[2] Anaximenes, the follower of Thales, like his master, was a bold and subtle reasoner, and called everything by its proper name. He denominated the one God Zeus, by which he intended to intimate that, like the air we

---

[1] Maur, Ind. Ant. cited from Diog. Laert., l. viii. p. 507.
[2] Euseb. de Præp. Evan., l. i. c. ult.

breathe, He is infinite, omnipresent, and eternal.[1] Xenophanes, the principal leader of the Eleatic sect, entertained the same belief; and described that Great Being, whom they all admitted to be incomprehensible, as "incorporeal, in substance, and figure *globular;* and in no respect similar to man. That He is all sight and hearing, but does not breathe. That He is all things; the mind and wisdom; not generate, but eternal, impassible, and immutable." Parmenides held that "the principle of all things is ONE; but that it is immovable." Sophocles assures us that in his time, the belief in one God, who made heaven and earth, was prevalent amongst those who had been initiated into the Greater mysteries.

Socrates and his pupil Plato maintained the same opinion. "By the name of God," said they, " we mean the parent of the world; the builder of the soul; the maker of heaven and earth; whom it is difficult to know by reason of His incredible power; and if known, it is impossible to clothe our knowledge in words." Anaxagoras

---

[1] The Emperor Trajan, in a conversation with the Rabbi Joshua, hearing the latter say that "God is everywhere present;" observed, "I should like to see Him." "God's presence is indeed everywhere," replied Joshua, "but He cannot be seen; no mortal eye can behold His glory." The Emperor insisted. "Well," said Joshua, "suppose we try first to look at one of His ambassadors." The Emperor consented. The Rabbi took him into the open air at noonday, and bid him look at the sun in its meridian splendour. "I cannot—the light dazzles me." "*Thou art unable,*" said Joshua, "*to endure the light of His creatures, and canst thou expect to behold the resplendent glory of the Creator?* Would not such a sight annihilate you?"—(Goodhugh's Lectures on Bibliographical Literature).

contended for the supreme government of one God, but acknowledged that he was unable to comprehend His nature. His pupil Euripides, however, was more fortunate, for he discovered the omnipresence of the Deity; and confesses it by asking whether it is possible to confine Him within the walls of a temple built with hands? Protagoras was banished by the Athenians for impiety, in declaring that "he knew nothing of the gods, because in so short a life it was impossible to acquire a knowledge of them."

The revolution of ages did not efface this profession of the divine unity, though it shook the credit of the Spurious Freemasonry, through whose medium it was conveyed. The solemn obligations, under the seal of which this great secret was communicated, proved but a slender tie upon the more sceptical philosophers, who felt little inclination to be satisfied with the popular reasons assigned for paying divine honours to a mixed multitude of deceased mortals. Cicero argues the being of a God from the regular structure of the universe; and Virgil, in his description of the process and end of initiation, winds up his detail with a view of the divine unity.

In like manner, Zeno taught the unity and eternity of the Deity. Plutarch, learned in all the rites and doctrines of the Spurious Freemasonry of Egypt and Greece, expresses himself plainly on this point in his treatise of Isis and Osiris. Aristides believed and taught his disciples that "Jove made all existing things, in the earth, the heavens, or the sea." Porphyry asserts that the oracle of Apollo commanded men to worship *deum generatorem et regem ante omnia, quem tremit cœlum et terra, atque mare, et infernorum abdita, et ipsa numina per horrescunt; quorum lex est Pater, quem, valde sancti honorant Hebræis.* Nor must I omit, in this brief enumeration of testimonies in proof of the admission of the divine unity amongst heathen nations, that remarkable expression which Lucian puts into the mouth of Cato: "God makes himself known to all the world; He fills up the whole circle of the universe, but *makes His particular abode in the centre,* which is the soul of the just."

Thus was the doctrine of the Monad or unity, the first Point in the Pythagorean Triangle, carried out in these early ages, and amongst an idolatrous people; for however they might worship an indefinite number of intelligences, they had discrimination enough to perceive that there could be only one Being of unbounded power, because a duplication of such beings would circumscribe the potency of each individual, and destroy his omnipotence and immutability. "It was idle," says Bryant, "in the ancients to make a disquisition about the identity of any god, as compared with another; and to adjudge him to Jupiter rather than to Mars, to Venus rather than Diana. According to Diodorus, some think that Osiris is Serapis; others that he is Dionusus; others still that he is Pluto; many take him for Zeus or Jupiter, and not a few for Pan. This was an unnecessary embarrassment; for *they were all titles of the same god;* there being originally by no means that diversity which is imagined, as Sir John Marsham has very justly observed. *Neque enim tanta πολυθεοτης. Gentium, quanta fuit deorum πολυωνυμια."* [1]

We shall see, however, in our examination of the Duad, that this belief, correct as it was in principle, admitted of some modification.

---

[1] Bryant, Anal., vol. i. p. 386.

THE DUAD OR LINE EXEMPLIFIED.

THE LINE, DUAD, DUALITY, OR THE NUMBER TWO.

CHAPTER II.

THE LINE.

DUAD, DUALITY, OR THE NUMBER TWO.

"THE next two points in the Pythagorean Triangle are denominated Duad, representing the number two, and answers to the geometrical Line, which, consisting of length without breadth, is bounded by two extreme points."—HEMMING'S LECTURES.

"The emblematical objects characteristic of the second degree of Masonry, are the two brazen pillars, the winding staircase, and the blazing star with the letter G *in the centre.*"—IBID.

THE twofold reason of diversity and inequality, and of everything that is divisible in mutation, and exists sometimes one way sometimes another, the Pythagoreans called DUAD, for the nature of the Duad in particular things is such. These reasons were not confined to the Italic sect, but other philosophers also have left certain unitive powers which comprise all things in the universe; and amongst them there are certain reasons of quality, dissimilitude, and diversity. Now these reasons, that the way of teaching might be more perspicuous, they called by the names of Monad and Duad; but it is all one amongst them if it be called biform, or equaliform, or diversiform."[1] Pierius, in his thirty-seventh book of Hieroglyphics, confirms this doctrine. He says, "*Ipse verò dualis numerus mystico significato* corpoream indicat naturam, et pro imanundis accipitur in sacris, quòd is numerus sociandis generandisque corporibus aptari solet. De quo videndus Adamantius lib. tertio in epistolam Pauli ad Romanos, ubi de propitiatorio loquitur. Summonet D. Hieron. in hanc sententiam adversus Jovinianum, animadvertendum esse juxta Hebraicam veritatem, in primo, et tertio, et quarto, et quinto, et sexto die, expletis operibus singulorum, subjectum esse, Et vidit Deus quòd esset bonum. In secundo verò die hoc omnino subtractum, ut admoneremur non esse bonum duplicem numerum, quòd ab unione dividat. Nam unitas tota Dei est, *dualitas verò significet hieroglyphicè fœdera nuptiarum*, quibus ubique Hieronymus paulò se infensiorem ostentat."

From such definitions and principles, it will not be difficult to see that the Duad was sufficiently comprehensive to admit of a vast number of references; and therefore the prolific fancy of poets and philosophers assigned to it a variety of remarkable qualities. Being even, it was esteemed an unlucky number, and dedicated to the malignant genii and the infernal deities, because it conveyed to the mind ideas of darkness, delusion, versa-

[1] Porph. Hist. Phil., p. 32.

tility, and unsteady conduct.[1] For this reason, the Pythagoreans spoke of two kinds of pleasure, "whereof that which indulgeth to the belly and to lasciviousness, by profusion of wealth, they compared to the murderous songs of the Syrens; the other, which consists in things honest and just, comprising all the necessary indulgences of life, is quite as attractive as the former, and does not bring repentance in its train."[2]

The Duad was considered indefinite and indeterminate, because no perfect figure can be made from two points only, which, if united, would merely become a right line; whence a notion was originated that it is defective in its principles, and superfluous in its application to the sciences. It signified also misfortune, from a general belief in its unpropitious qualities; and discord, because in music that which renders dissonances grating, is, that the sounds which form them, instead of uniting to produce harmony, are heard each by itself as two distinct sounds, though produced at one and the same time. Brand tells us,[3] that there is a little history extant of the unfortunate reigns of William II., Henry II., Edward II., Richard II., Charles II., and James II., entitled "Numerus Infaustus;" in the preface to which the author says, "Such of the kings of England as were the *Second* of any name, proved very unfortunate princes."

The number two was referred to several of the female deities, and particularly to Juno, because

[1] Porph. vit. Pyth., p. 84.   [2] Ibid., p. 25.   [3] Pop. Ant., vol. iii. p. 145.

she was the *sister* and *wife* of Jove;[1] and hence the Duad became a symbol of marriage. On this subject Hierocles says, two things are necessary to all men, in order to pass through life in a becoming manner, viz., the aid of kindred, and sympathetic benevolence. But we cannot find anything more sympathetic than a wife, nor anything more kindred than children, both of which are afforded by marriage. And to produce these two beneficial effects, Callicratides gives the following excellent advice: "Wedlock should be coadapted to the peculiar tone of the soul, so that the husband and wife may not only accord with each other in prosperous, but also in adverse fortune. It is requisite, therefore, that the husband should be the regulator, master, and preceptor of his wife. The regulator, indeed, in paying diligent attention to her affairs; but the master, in governing and exercising authority over her; and the preceptor in teaching her such things as it is fit for her to know."

But how unfortunate soever the Duad may have been esteemed as a general principle, it was not devoid of its share of beneficent properties to balance against those that were malignant or forbidding. "The two principles," said the Paracelsic Lectures of Continental Masonry, "are not always at strife, but sometimes in league with each other, to produce good. Thus death and anguish are the cause of Fire, but fire is the cause of Life. To the abyss it gives sting and

---

[1] Mart. Capel. Eulog. in somn. Scip.

fierceness, else there would be no mobility. To the Light—world, essence, else there would be no production but an eternal Arcanum. To the world it gives both essence and springing, whence it becomes the cause of all things." The Duad was defined by the Pythagoreans, " the only principle of purity; yet not even, nor evenly even, nor unevenly even, nor evenly uneven." It was an emblem of fortitude and courage, and taught that as a man ought to do no wrong, neither ought he to suffer any, without a due sense and modest resentment of it; and therefore, according to Plutarch, the " Ephori laid a mulct upon Sciraphidas, because he tamely submitted to many injuries and affronts, concluding him perfectly insensible to his own interest, as he did not boldly and honestly vindicate his reputation from the wrongs and aspersions which had been cast upon it; under the impression that he would be equally dull and listless in the defence of his country, if it should be attacked by a hostile invader."

I have already observed that the centre was a representation of the Monad; but according to the doctrines promulgated by the Theosophical Masons of the last century, it produced several dualities; for the centre was explained by them as the *Verbum fiat*, the natural Word of God, the maker of all creatures in the inward and outward worlds. The same Word hath out of the Fire, the Light, and the Darkness, made itself material, moving, and perceptible, out of which existed the third principle, the visible world, the life and substance whereof is come out of the eternal nature the Fire, and out of the great mystery, the Light, also out of the Darkness, which is the separator of Fire and Light, Love and Enmity, Good and Evil, Joy and Pain." And they went on to say, that there are two sorts of Fire, and two sorts of Light, which they explained mystically.

The Duad was elevated by the ancient philosophers of the Italic sect into a symbol of Justice, because of its two equal parts. Hence Archytas, who was a follower of Pythagoras, says, "The manners and pursuits of the citizens should be deeply tinctured with justice; for this will cause them to be sufficient to themselves, and will be the means of distributing to each of them that which is due to him according to his desert. For thus also the sun, moving in a circle through the zodiac, distributes to everything on the earth, generation, nutriment, and an appropriate portion of life; administering, as if it were a just and equitable legislation, the excellent temperature of the seasons."[1]

It signified also science, because the demonstration of an unknown number or fact is produced from syllogistic reasonings on some other number or fact which is known; and this is deducible by the aid of science. It was further considered as a symbol of the soul, which is said to be divided into two parts, the rational and the irrational;

[1] Fragments of Archytas, p. 16.

the latter being subdivided into the irascible and the appetitive. The rational part enables us to arrive at the truth by contemplation and judgment; while the irrational uniformly impels the soul to evil. And it signified Opinion, which must be either true or false; and Harmony, whence the ancients introduced music at their banquets along with wine; that by its harmonious order and soothing effect it might prove an antidote to the latter, which being drank intemperately, renders both mind and body imbecile.

In the science of astronomy there are two nodes, called the dragon's head and tail; and in astrology the aspects are of two kinds, dexter and sinister, according as they are agreeable with, or contrary to, the succession of the Signs; and the Duad referred particularly to the moon by reason of her two horns when at the change. In the first chapter of Genesis the Duad is applied to the Sun and Moon; which are there termed "the two great Lights, the former to rule the day and the latter to rule the night;"[1] and mystically signified the light of time. Freemasonry has added a third. It will be observed, however, that the sun and moon are called great lights, partly from their nature and effects; because they give more light than other stars. The sun appeareth alone in the day, not because he is alone, but because, through his exceeding brightness, the other stars cannot be seen. The moon also in her brightness obscureth many stars; and being more

[1] Gen. i. 16.

beautiful than any other, hath worthily the chief pre-eminence in ruling the night.[1]

The Pythagorean philosophy, says Reuchlin,[2] taught that the Monad and Duad were a symbol of the principles of the universe; "for when we make inquiry into the causes and origin of all things, what sooner occurs than one and two? That which we first behold with our eyes is the same, and not another; that which we first conceive in our mind is Identity and Alterity—one and two. Alcmæon affirmed *two* to be many, which, he said, were contrarieties, yet unconfined and indefinite, as white and black, sweet and bitter, good and evil, great and small. These multiplicitous diversities the Pythagoreans designed by the number Ten, as proceeding from the Duad; viz., finite and infinite, even and odd, one and many, right and left, male and female, steadfast and moved, straight and crooked, light and darkness, square and oblong. These pairs are *two*, and therefore contrary; they are reduced all into ten, that being the most perfect number, as containing more kinds of numeration than the rest: even, odd; square, cube; long, plain; the first uncompounded, and first compounded, than which nothing is more absolute, since in ten proportions four cubic numbers are consummated, of which all things consist.

"Categories, reducible to two, Substance and Accident, both springing from one essence; for ten so loves two, that from one it proceeds to two,

---

[1] Aquin. ex Chrys. Hom., vi.　　　[2] A. Cabal., l. ii.

and by two it reverts into one. The first Ternary is of one and two, not compounded but consistent; one having no position, makes no composition; an unit, whilst an unit, hath no position, nor a point whilst a point. There being nothing before one, we rightly say, one is first; two is not compounded of numbers, but a co-ordination of units only. It is therefore the first number, being the first multitude; not commensurable by any number, but by a unit, the common measure of all number; for one, two, is nothing but two; so that the multitude which is called Triad, arithmeticians term the first number uncompounded, the Duad being not an uncompounded number, but rather not compounded."

The Chinese philosophers entertained similar fancies about the colour of blue, which is formed by a mixture of red and black. This colour, they say, "being the colour of heaven, represents the active and passive principle reunited in one; the male and female, the obscure and brilliant. All corporeal beings are produced by inapprehensible nature, emanating from blue, which forms the origin of all subtile natures."[1] In the science of astrology, which was very prevalent half a century ago, the signs were invested with significant colours. Thus it was said that Taurus was designated by white mixed with citron; Aries and Gemini, by white and red; Cancer, green and russet; Leo, red and green; Virgo, black speckled with blue; Libra, black or dark

[1] Colebrook, Philosophy of the Hindus, p. 21.

crimson; Scorpio, brown; Sagittarius, yellow or green; Capricorn, black or russet; Aquarius, a sky colour or blue; and Pisces by a brilliant white.

Nor were the Jews destitute of a respect for the number two; which was indeed inculcated in the Mosaical writings. Thus while the clean beasts were admitted into the ark of Noah by sevens, the unclean ones were allowed to enter only by pairs. The angels that were deputed to destroy Sodom were two; Lot had two daughters; the sons of Isaac and the daughters of Laban were each two in number, as were also the sons of Joseph. Moses was directed to make two cherubim; the Onyx-stones of remembrance on the high priest's shoulders were two, to symbolise the Sun and Moon, as Josephus says; but Beda thinks they were emblematical of the faith and practice of the patriarchs and prophets, while others suppose, with greater probability, that the high priest bore them on his shoulders to prefigure the manner in which Christ was to bear the sins of His people. The Jewish offerings were frequently directed to be by pairs; as two lambs, two pigeons, two turtles, two kids, &c. The waive loaves were two; and the shewbread was placed on the table in two rows; the silver trumpets to direct the march of the Israelites in the wilderness were the same number.

Again, Joshua erected two monuments on passing the river Jordan, one in the bed of the river, and the other on its banks; the temples of Solomon and of Gaza were each supported on two pillars; Jeroboam made two golden calves, and set them up at Dan and Bethel; there were two witnesses against Naboth, as the Mosaic law required in cases affecting human life; and two bears were sent to vindicate the character of Elisha. In the case of Naaman the Syrian, we find the use of this number fully exemplified in the two mules' burden of earth—two young men of the sons of the prophets—two talents—two changes of garments—two servants, &c. In the visions of Daniel the ram had two horns; and in Zachariah we have two olive-trees, two anointed ones, and two staves called Beauty and Bands, an emblem of brotherhood. Similar coincidences might be found in the Gospels, but the detail would be tedious, and the result without utility, as far as regards Freemasonry.

In our system, the principle of the duad is plainly enunciated (although two is not esteemed a masonic number) in the two Pillars of the Porch of Solomon's Temple, which were placed in that situation by the wise and judicious monarch, to commemorate the remarkable pillar of a cloud and of fire; the former of which proved a light and guide to the Israelites in their escape from their Egyptian oppression; the other represents the cloud which proved the destruction of Pharaoh and his host in their attempt to follow them through the depths of the Red Sea. Our noble and illustrious Grand Master placed them in this conspicuous situation that the Jews might have that memorable event in their recollection, both in going in and coming out from divine worship.

These two famous pillars did not stand insulated or detached from the building, but were applied to the useful purpose of supporting the entablature of the pronaos. They were of cast brass, and their dimensions, use, and ornaments are particularly described in the Fellow Craft's Lecture. The chapiters represented the system of the creation; and the balls by which they were surmounted, the celestial and terrestrial globes. The network denoting the strong and beautiful texture of all created things; the chain-work, the different and complicated evolutions of the several systems, moving with regularity through the vast expanse, and revolving on their own axes; the opening flowers denote the mild and genial influence of the fixed stars; and the pomegranate, the secret and unknown power by which the universe is sustained. Their height reminds us of the two Grand Master Hirams; while the sphere and cylinder are sublime and significant emblems, which contain the principles of the two higher branches of Geometry.

In the spurious Freemasonry of some ancient nations, this principle of duality was extended to support the doctrine of a good and evil power, who possessed almost equal government in this lower world; and the prosperity or decadence of a nation was supposed to be produced by the superiority of one or other of these beings, which, however, was esteemed, in most cases, accidental. In Persia the doctrine attained its climax. Oromases was Light, and Ahriman, Darkness. Hyde says, "The first Magi did not look upon the two principles as co-eternal, but believed that light was eternal, and that darkness was produced in time; and the origin of this evil principle they account for in this manner: Light can produce nothing but light, and can never be the origin of evil; how then was evil produced? Light, they say, produced several beings, all of them spiritual, luminous, and powerful; but their chief, whose name was Ahriman, had an evil thought contrary to the light. He doubted, and by that doubting he became dark. From hence proceeded all evils, dissension, malice, and everything also of a contrary nature to the light. These two principles made war upon one another, till at last peace was concluded, upon condition that the lower world should be in subjection to Ahriman for seven thousand years; after which space of time, he is to surrender back the world to the Light."[1]

In countries where the two principles were represented by two serpents, the solstitial colures were described under these symbols. Thus, in the Egyptian hieroglyphics, two serpents intersecting each other at right angles, upon a globe, denoted the earth. These rectangular intersections were at the solstitial points.[2] The Teutonic

[1] Hyde, Rel. Ant. Pers., c. ix. p. 163.
[2] Jablonski, Panth. Eg., l. i. c. 4, cited by Deane, p. 73.

Masonry of the last century thus explained the two principles of Light and Darkness. "From the eternal centre is made the eternal substantiality as a body or weakness, being a sinking down, and the spirit is a springing up, whence comes motion, penetration, and multiplication; and when the spirit created the substantiality into an image, breathing the spirit of the Trinity into it, the whole essences, even all forms of nature, the power of Light and Darkness, and the whole eternity, it instantly blossomed and became the paradise or angelical world. In the Darkness is the genetrix, in the Light is the wisdom; the first imaged by devils, the other by angels, as a similitude of the whole eternal being, to speak as a creature. And Lucifer imaging beyond the meekness of the Trinity, kindled in himself the matrix of Fire, and that of nature becoming corporeal, then was the second form of the matrix, viz., the meekness of the substantiality enkindled, whence water originated, out of which was made an heaven to captivate the fire, and of that Fire and Water came the Stars."

Other Oriental nations carry their belief of good and evil genii (Jinns), who are for ever contending against each other; the one to extend the dominion of vice, and the other that of virtue. The beautiful fictions in the Arabian Nights Entertainments are founded on this belief. The origin of the Jinn is thus given by Lane from El-Kaziveenee. "It is related in histories, that a race of Jinn in ancient times, before the creation of

Adam, inhabited the earth, and covered it, the land and the sea, and the plains and the mountains; and the favours of God were multiplied upon them, and they had government, and prophecy, and religion, and law; but they transgressed and offended, and opposed their prophets, and made wickedness to abound in the earth; whereupon God, whose name be exalted, sent against them an army of angels, who took possession of the earth, and drove away the Jinn to the regions of the islands, and made many of them prisoners; and of those who were made prisoners was Azazeel, afterwards called Iblees, from his despair." The Jinnee have fire circulating in their veins in the place of blood; and when any of them receives a mortal wound this fire generally consumes him to ashes. When they appear to mankind it is usually in some hideous form.

The legend of the Spurious Freemasonry is founded on the above principle of duality. It speaks of a good and evil power, the former being destroyed by the machinations of the latter; and after a variety of adventures, the body is found and restored to life. This gives vivacity to another form of the duad. The aphanism and euresis were both celebrated during the initiations; lamentation and sorrow marking the first, as a sacrifice due to the immolated deity; while the last was a season of rejoicing at his recovery; and the formula was—"Rejoice, ye Mystæ, for your god is found!" And the legend was the same in all material points, whether the celebrations were in honour of Osiris, Adonis, Bacchus, or the deity of any other country; and the duality was still further extended by the supposition that the wife of the dismembered god was the individual deputed to search for the body. The reference was preserved as well in Osiris and Typhon as in Osiris and Isis, and the corresponding deities in every nation of the earth.

The superstition, which was so common throughout all antiquity, of realising the duality by combining the worship of the serpent with that of a tree, or offering rites to the Ophite deity in a sacred grove, originated with the paradisiacal serpent and tree of knowledge. This united worship is depicted on the sepulchral monuments of the Greeks and Romans, on the coins of Tyre, and among the Fetiches of Whidah. We shall find them, in the same union, pervading the religion of the Hyperboreans of every description, the superstition of the Scandinavians, and the worship of the Druids.[1]

Pythagoras, in his system, enunciated the dual principle in the exoteric and esoteric character of the mysteries. The candidates for admission were strictly examined respecting their moral character; and if they bore the test, they were admitted as exoterics, which continued five years, during which period they were subjected to very serious trials, both bodily and mental, and doomed to a perpetual silence; and afterwards they were made

[1] Dean., Serpent, p. 231.

esoterics, and permitted to see the Master, which they had never yet been allowed to do, although they had heard him deliver his lectures on the outside of the screen. If they were rejected, they were looked upon as dead, and a tomb was erected to their memory.

Again, the form of instruction used by this philosopher was twofold; and his disciples passed under the denomination of the Acousmatici and the Mathematici. The former were instructed only in the elements, and the latter in the more elaborate and secret principles of science. And Pythagoras taught, still adhering to the principle of the duad, that every man was placed between virtue and vice, like the lower part of the letter Y. As there can be none happy before their death, so none is to be esteemed unhappy whilst he lives. But if at his death he is burdened with vice, his misery then begins. This misery the philosopher divided into two kinds; some, he said, would ultimately be delivered from punishment, others would endure infinite pain everlastingly. Again, he taught that there are two mansions in the lower regions, one called Elysium, for those who will ultimately ascend into heaven; and Tartarus, for those who are never to be delivered from torment. On the other hand, those who have chosen the path of virtue, who have lived piously, and died in peace, shall ascend into the transparent ether, and live with the blessed as gods.

In Christian philosophy, the duad is equally

esteemed, because it includes the entire essence of the system, as expounded by its divine author, who possessed two natures, and was comprehended in two great moral precepts, the love of God and our neighbour. For the same reason, Christianity has two sacraments, and a divine symbol of two united equilateral triangles, to figure the two natures of Christ. It represents man in a twofold state, as referring to time and eternity; teaches that the future will have two places of reward and punishment, which are attained by two preparatory steps, death and judgment. The two great covenants or dispensations, represented by Isaac and Ishmael, are symbolised in Freemasonry by a most beautiful type. Thus, St Paul says,— "Abraham had two sons, the one by a bondmaid, the other by a free woman. But he who was of the bond woman was born after the flesh; but he of the free woman was by promise. Which things are an allegory; for these are the two covenants; the one from Mount Sinai, which gendereth to bondage, which is Hagar. For this Hagar is Mount Sinai, in Arabia, and answereth to Jerusalem which now is, and is in bondage with her children; but Jerusalem which is above is FREE, which is the mother of us all."[1]

Here we have a plain exposition of the two covenants, the Law and the Gospel, the first of which was a shadow of the second. "Howbeit that was not first which was spiritual, but that

[1] Gal. iv. 22-26.

which was natural, and afterward that which was spiritual; the first man is of the earth, earthy; the second man is the Lord from heaven."[1] Our first estate is Time, our second Eternity. The same beautiful allegory is kept up from the time of the first prophecy relative to the two seeds; and as it was then with Cain and Abel, he that was born after the flesh persecuted him that was born after the Spirit. It appears, then, to have been understood not only by Moses and Solomon, but by all other holy men of old, that the two colours of the Mosaic pavement, black and white, were a figure of the divine and human nature of Him who was in the pillar of a cloud and of fire, the Redeemer of His people from Egyptian bondage.

In like manner, there are two witnesses mentioned by St John in the Book of Revelation (Rev. xi. 3), which is in strict accordance with customs of great antiquity; as Moses and Aaron in Egypt, Elijah and Elisha in the apostasy of the ten tribes, and Zerubbabel and Jeshua after the Babylonish captivity, to whom these two witnesses are particularly compared. Our Saviour sent forth His disciples by two and two; and Bishop Newton has observed, that the principal Reformers have usually appeared as it were in pairs, as the Waldenses and Albigenses, John Huss and Jerome of Prague, Luther and Calvin, Cranmer and Ridley, and their followers.

[1] 1 Cor. xv. 46, 47.

One great principle of the duality is in the formation of the sexes, for the propagation of each particular species of man and beast. The cabalistic Jews had some curious ideas respecting the origin of male and female in the human subject. The Rabbi Samuel bar Nachman held, with many other of his brethren, that woman was jointly created with man; being attached to his back; so that the figure of Adam was double, one part before being man, and the other part behind being woman; and he subsequently says that God separated this back figure from man. This opinion is adopted by Jarchi, Aben Ezra, R. Bechayai, Eliezer Askenasi, and Isaac Caro, in their commentaries, who all agree that by the words "male and female created He them," is to be understood literally that Adam and Eve were created together in one form, which was called Adam, and signifies both male and female.[1]

The lectures of the old German Rose Croix contain a curious application of the duad, which was adopted by M. Peuvret into his Paracelsic degrees. It is as follows :—" Adam, seeing two divine forms in himself, one paradisiacal, *within* himself, the other *without* him, he thought to eat of both, viz., the paradisiacal and the mixed of good and evil, till he sunk into a sleep, which signifies death, where the spirit of this world formed him into such a man as we now are, and

---

[1] See a great deal more on this subject in the "Conciliator of the Rabbi Manassah ben Israel," vol. i. p. 17.

Eve into a woman; and when they had eaten, the spirit of this world captivated their souls; their essences were earthy, their flesh and blood bestial, so that they begat children in two kingdoms, viz., of Wrath and Love, the first a murderer, the second holy; for the word of grace and covenant had, on their fall, set itself in the light of their life."

ILLUSTRATION OF THE TRIAD, OR SUPERFICE.

THE SUPERFICE, OR EQUILATERAL TRIANGLE, TRIAD, TERNARY, OR THE NUMBER THREE.

CHAPTER III.

THE SUPERFICE, OR EQUILATERAL TRIANGLE.

TRIAD, TERNARY, OR THE NUMBER THREE.

> "Tres imbris torti radios, tres nubis aquosæ
> Addiderant; rutili tres ignis, et alitis Austri;
> Fulgores nunc terrificos, sonitumque metumque
> Miscebant operi, flammisque sequacibus iras."
> VIRGIL.

> "THE three Sojourners represent the three Stones on which the three Grand Masters kneeled to offer up their prayers for the success of the work; and hereby we have a lesson that in everything we undertake, we ought to offer up our prayers to the Almighty for a blessing on our labours."—OLD R. A. LECTURE.

THE Pythagoreans maintained the principle of three worlds and pronounced the third infinite; for they thought that the triad embraced all matter. These three worlds were denominated the inferior, the superior, and the supreme. The inferior contains bodies and magnitudes, as the guardians of things generated and consequently corruptible. Next above is the superior world, intended for superior powers, called by Pythagoras in his Golden Verses, the immortal gods, produced by the divine Mind. The third world, called supreme, is the abode of the One Great Deity, who existed from eternity, and has the sole government of the world. These three worlds were called receptacles; the first of quantity; the second of intelligences; the third of principles; the first circumscriptively, the second definitively, and the third repletively. But the ternary or triad was not only accounted a sacred number amongst the Pythagoreans, but also as containing some mystery in nature was therefore made use of by other Greeks and Pagans in their religious rites; for Aristotle says distinctly that the number three was taken from nature as an observation of its laws, as the most proper to be used in sacrificing to the gods and other purifications. (De Cælo., l. 1, c. 5.)

The triad was esteemed the first perfect number, and hence oracles were delivered from a tripod. It was denominated by way of eminence, the mystical number; and both Socrates and Plato acknowledge three principles of things, God, Idea, and Matter: which had been already symbolised by Pythagoras in three secret figures, viz., Infinite, One, and Two; the former was the way in which he designated the supreme Deity; by unity he meant form; and by alterity, matter; infinite, in the supreme world; one, in the intellectual; and two, in the sensible. The peace and concord which spring from happy marriages, was represented by the triad; whence probably it was designated, in the notation of the Chinese, by the figure of *a point within a circle*. The Pythagoreans taught the duties which appertain to a man and his wife, in order to secure the three blessings of a married state. The things, say they, "which are peculiar to a man are three, viz., to lead an army, to govern, and to speak in public. The offices peculiar to a woman are also three in number; *i.e.*, to be the guardian of a house, to stay at home, and to be attentive to the comforts of her husband. And the virtues which make the married state happy, appertain equally to them both; and these are FORTITUDE, JUSTICE, and PRUDENCE. For it is fit that both the husband and the wife should possess the virtues of the body and the soul ; health, strength, and beauty. Fortitude and Prudence pertain to the man, while TEMPERANCE belongs peculiarly to the woman."

Like the duad, this number was emblematical of justice. Pierius affirms that "ut verò trini prosequamur significata, ternarium veteres, ut alibi etiam ostendimus, Justitiæ dedicarunt, ut de Pythagoricis disciplinis Plutarchus ait. Injuria siquidem afficere, neque non affici, cum extrema sint, et idcirco vitiosa, justum equaliter utrinque reductum in medio residet. Sanè Pythagorici non numerus tantùm, verùm etiam figuras deorum nominibus dedicarunt; quippe qui triangulum equilaterum Minervam appellabant.

Verticigenam et Tritogeniam propterea, quòd tribus perpendicularibus lineis ab angulis tribus dissecetur."[1] To the above explanation Pierius has subjoined these figures—

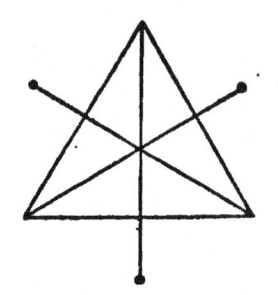

The triad was said to be a connective and collective communion, as the symbol of justice, because it is that disposition of the soul which adapts itself to those that are near us. "For as rhythm is to motion, and harmony to the voice, so is justice to communion; since it is the common good of those that govern, and those that are governed, because it co-harmonises political society. But equity and benignity are certain assessors of justice: the former softening the severity of punishment, and the latter extending pardon to less guilty offenders."[2] The same number also inculcated the wisdom derivable from prudence, because men, looking forward to the *future*, conduct themselves at *present* by experience of the *past*. And prudence was defined "the faculty of disposing all the accidents of life so as to produce human happiness. Thus we value medicine, not so much for the love of

---

[1] Pier. Hier., fo. 292.
[2] Diotogenes in Taylor's Fragments, p. 25.

science, as for the promotion of health; neither would prudence be desirable, if it were not the medium through which happiness may be obtained. By prudence we provide against anything which may afflict either the body or the mind. Under its governance we are enabled to keep within compass, to extinguish the ardour of all unruly desires, and live in peace and tranquillity. The prudent person alone, being contented to live within due bounds, avoids all error, ignorance, and discontent, which produce the troubles and afflictions that bear down other men."[1]

Pythagoras entertained an idea that all human virtues not only proceed from this number but absolutely depend upon it; and he particularly mentions temperance. And for this reason, Socrates advises us to beware of such meats as persuade a man though he be not hungry to eat them; and of those drinks that would prevail with him to swallow them when he is not thirsty. Not that he absolutely forbade their use, but that we might abstain from them, when they were not necessary; for that which is delightful to nature as a matter of nourishment, is alone proper for it. He that is hungry may eat things either necessary or pleasant; but when he is freed from his natural appetite, he ought not to raise up a fresh one.

The Jewish cabalists had a curious opinion respecting the application of this number in the

[1] Epicurus, in Stanley's Philosophy, vol. iii. p. 3, c. 8.

case of the three holy men mentioned by Ezekiel (xiv. 14), each of whom they say was witness to the creation, destruction, and restoration of the world. Noah saw the earth reduced to chaos, and after the flood restored to its primitive state. Daniel saw his country, Jerusalem (a world in miniature), entirely destroyed; and in his days flourish again by the rebuilding of the Temple. In like manner Job saw his house and family (a small world to him) destroyed, and afterwards become prosperous. The prophet, they add, names these three for their constancy and firmness when tried: Noah without fear of being killed, building an ark in which he intended to save only himself; Job against Satan; and Daniel in the lions' den. He names them also from having escaped the three evils—sword, famine, and wild beasts. Thus Noah was preserved from ferocious animals in the ark; from the famine that happened in his time; and from the sword with which men tried to kill him when they saw that he alone would escape at the deluge. Job escaped famine; the sword which, he said, cleaveth my veins asunder; and from the wild beasts of his country. Daniel escaped famine during the three years when Nebuchadnezzar besieged Jerusalem; the sword when he was taken prisoner, and lastly from the lions.[1]

The triad was said to be the cause of wisdom and understanding, from its application to the

[1] Concil., vol. ii. p. 211.

three sciences of Music, Geometry, and Astronomy. Thus the harmonic triad in music is compounded of three radical sounds consisting of a fundamental note, its third, and its fifth; the latter of which is divided into two thirds by different processes. First *harmonically;* as when the greater third is lowest, in which case the triad is said to be perfect and natural. Secondly *arithmetically;* when the lesser third is lowest; and then the triad is called flat or imperfect.[1] In the two latter sciences Pythagoras affirmed that the cube of three has the power of the lunar circle, because the moon goes round her orb in twenty-seven days.

In the Hermesian system, the ineffable secrets were reputed to have been transmitted through three patriarchs only, viz., Adam, Seth, and Enoch; the latter of whom was identified with Hermes himself, the founder of the spurious Freemasonry of Egypt. Cudworth observes that "since all these three, Orpheus, Pythagoras, and Plato, travelling in Egypt, were there initiated in that arcane theology of the Egyptians called Hermaical, it seemeth probable that this doctrine of a divine triad was also part of the arcane theology of the Egyptians. It hath been also noted that there were some footsteps of such a trinity in the Mithraic mysteries amongst the Persians, derived from Zoroaster; as likewise that it was expressly contained in the magic or Chaldaic oracles, of whatsoever authority they

---

[1] Busby, Dict. Mus. in voc.

may be. Moreover, it hath been signified that the Samothracians had very anciently a certain trinity of gods, that were the highest of all their gods, and that called by an Hebrew name too, Cabbirim, or the mighty gods; and that from thence the Roman Capitoline trinity of gods was derived."

The triad of master and wardens, which distinguishes our system of Freemasonry, are the legitimate repository of its secrets, and bear a reference to certain attributes of the Deity. This triad is not peculiar to Freemasonry, but had a corresponding application in the spurious system of India. Wisdom was represented by the symbol of a circle of heads; Strength by the elephant; and Beauty by horns, or a nimbus formed by the solar rays. The great deity of India, Siva or Maha Deo, is frequently depicted with three eyes, denoting the past, present, and future, and thus constituting a symbol of prudence. In general, his name is compounded of the triad Cal-Agni-Rudra, or Time—Fire—Fate.

The French philosophers who contributed so much to deteriorate genuine Freemasonry about a century ago, affected to entertain a profound respect for the mysterious institutions of antiquity, and comprehended the doctrine of the Pagan cosmogonies, compared with that related by Moses, under the form of two triads—viz., the exoteric, consisting of Buddha—Revelation—Church; and the esoteric of intellect—Logos—Great Union. And in their cabalistic jargon, three was called "the mystical number;" and the square of three "the number evolving itself." The three mystical properties, they went on to say in their theosophic lectures, "which constitute the essence of the world, consist of sulphur, mercury, and salt. *Sul* is the free *lubet* of the eternal abyss; in the internal, *sul* is God, and *phur* is nature—viz., the Eternal Nature—a hard attraction, the case of fire; and *sul* the cause of the lustre in the fire; but the light riseth not in the sulphur alone, but in mercury is the dividing made, and its true real body is *sal*. The astringency makes gross stones; mercury and the lubet metals. And of the freeing from the wrath by the light and meekness come the precious stones, gold, &c., for all things consist in these three forms, sulphur, mercury, and sal."

Sir Walter Scott, in his notes to the "Lay of the Last Minstrel," has adduced a legend to show the influence of the number three, even amongst the aerial beings who were supposed to possess superhuman powers. He said, "There were two men, late in the evening, when it was growing dark, employed in fastening their horses upon the common, when they heard a voice, at some distance, crying *tint, tint, tint*, three times. One of the men, named Moffat, called out, 'What deil has tint you? Come here.' Immediately a creature appeared, in something like the human form. It was surprisingly little, distorted in features and misshapen in limbs. As soon as the two men could see it plainly, they ran home in a great fright, imagining they had met with some goblin. By the way Moffat fell, and it ran over him, and was at home at the house as soon as either of them, and stayed there a long time. One evening, when the women were milking the cows in the loan, it was playing among the children near by them, when suddenly they heard a loud, shrill voice cry Gilpin Horner! *three times;* when it started and said, 'That is me, I must away,' and instantly disappeared, and was never heard of more." This being was an imp, and not a fairy, which latter were somewhat obstinately attached to *even* numbers.

The number three was incorporated into the religious ceremonies of all nations. Among the Romans, says Borlase,[1] "Corineus went three times round the assembly at Misenus's funeral to purify them; three times was the effigy of a coy lover to be drawn round the altar to inspire him with love. In the festival called the Amburvalia, the victim was to be led round the fields three times. In the sacrifices of Bacchus, the priestesses were to go three times round the altar with dishevelled hair. Among the Greeks, three times did Medea, in imitation of the Bacchæ, go round the aged Æson with fire; three times with water; and three times with sulphur; and when she was about to invoke the three powers of the night, her goddess Hecate, the moon, the stars, and all the inferior deities resident in the elements of nature, three times she turned herself about. The

[1] Ant. Cor., p. 131.

description of her, the stillness of the night, the propriety of the addresses, and parts of her prayer, are all extremely poetical—

> Ter se convertit, ter sumptis flumine crinem
> Irroravit aquis, ternis ululatibus ora
> Solvit, et in durâ submisso poplite terrâ,
> Nox, ait, &c.[1]

The names of the Pythagorean triad are legion. I enumerate a few of them from Stanley:—Saturnia, Latona, Cornucopia, Ophion, Thetis, Harmonia, Hecate, Erana, Charitia, Polyhymnia, Pluto, Arctus, Lichelice, Damatrame, Discordia, Metis, Tridume, Triton, President of the Sea, Tritogenia, Achelous, Nactis, Agyiopeza, Curetis, Cratæis, Symbenia, Mariadge, Gorgonia, Phorcia, Trisamus, Lydius. From hence it will be evident that the philosophers attached so much veneration to the number three, as to extend its supernatural influence to every object in the creation. It was necessary to the success of every undertaking, and without its aid, a disgraceful failure was sure to be the inevitable result.

The application of this number in our system of Freemasonry is equally extensive, although the reasons for it are inadequately explained in the lectures. In one of the oldest known formulas, we find three degrees, three chief officers, three movable and three immovable jewels, three knocks, three pillars, three working tools, &c., but no reason is assigned why this peculiarity had been

[1] Ovid, Met., lvii. 182–190.

adopted. In another ritual, used later in the century, it is applied to the Holy Trinity, and the three Grand Masters at the building of Solomon's Temple. And in the lectures of Hemming and Shadbolt, reference is given to the three great interior senses or elements of human intellect; the first of which is *perception*, the cause of simple ideas or impressions received from external objects, without any active exertions of the intellectual powers. The second is *judgment*, or the faculty of digesting, comparing, and reasoning upon these simple ideas. The third is *volition*, or the conclusion which results from the operations of judgment, and concentrates the whole energy of the mind in a fixed and certain point.

Freemasonry contains another beautiful illustration of the number three, which ought not to be overlooked. It alludes to an ancient and venerable exhortation in the Sacred Scriptures—"Ask, and you shall have—Seek, and you shall find—Knock, and it shall be opened unto you." These words were uttered by Him who spake as never man spake; and as He has thus constituted a passport into an earthly Lodge, so also must He be our passport into a Lodge not made with hands, eternal in the heavens.

M. Fustier, the inventor of a new system of Masonry on the Continent, introduced into his lectures, from the theories of Behmen and other theosophical visionaries, a dissertation on three principles of Light, all of which are eternal.

"The first was such a light as is produced by darkness; the second a meek and loving light, but still majestic and potent; the third resulting from fire and light, brings perfect happiness, both in this world and that which is to come. Thus the stars figure God in His infinity and eternity, according to the first principle; in His majestic kingdom of Light, according to the second; and in His gracious kingdom of Love, according to the third. And they are, in the third principle, the express word of what the devils are in the dark abyss, and of what the holy angels are in the heavenly world."

Des Etangs has promulgated an opinion which requires to be seriously considered before it is adopted as an undeniable truth—that the legitimate epochs in Masonry are three; the first comprehending all antiquity from the establishment of the famous Lodges in India, whence the science passed to Egypt, and from thence to Italy and Greece, and its secret mysteries were applied to government and religion. The second period commenced with the advent of Christ; and its principles inspired the first Christians with brotherly love, and the theological and cardinal virtues, and furnished them with equanimity and resolution to undergo sufferings the most excruciating, and deaths the most severe. The third epoch was coeval, according to this theory, with the revival of letters, and has continued to the times in which we live.

It will be unnecessary to point out the numerous

triad references[1] which occur in the mechanism and lectures of our system of Freemasonry, because they have been already expatiated on at large in Lecture ix. of the author's Historical Landmarks of the Order.

The mysteries of heathenism imitated this triple principle; and in the religious services of Delphi, when the priestess of Apollo delivered her oracles, she sat upon a tripod, which Athenæus calls "the tripod of truth." This was a name commonly given to any sort of vessel or table which was supported upon three feet. The tripod of the Pythian priestess was distinguished by a base emblematical of her god, consisting of a triple-headed serpent of brass, whose body, folded in circles growing wider and wider towards the ground, formed a conical column; and it is well known that the cone was sacred to the solar deity. The three heads were disposed triangularly, in order to sustain the three feet of the tripod, which was of gold. Herodotus tells us that it was consecrated to Apollo by the Greeks, out of the spoils of the Persians after the battle of Platæa.

---

[1] It may be remarked here as a note, that our British Solomon, King James, broached a triad of what he esteemed detestable things, unfit for human beings. "His Majesty professed that were he to invite the devil to a dinner, he should provide these three dishes. 1. A roasted pig. 2. A poll of ling and mustard. And 3. A pipe of tobacco for digestion."—(Apophthegms of King James, p. 4.)

[2] See this subject more fully treated on in Dean's Worship of the Serpent, p. 198.

The British Druids, some of whose rites and institutions, according to the opinion of Hutchinson and other ancient brethren, "were probably retained in forming the ceremonies of Masonry," had a peculiar veneration for this number; and arranged the classes both in their civil and religious polity upon ternary principles. Nothing could be transacted without a reference to this number. On solemn occasions, the processions were formed three times round the sacred enclosure of Caer Sidi; their invocations were thrice repeated; and even their poetry was composed in triads. The ternary deiscal, or procession from east to west by the south, accompanied all their rites, whether civil or ecclesiastical; and nothing was accounted sanctified without the performance of this preliminary ceremony. The tenets of their religion were founded on three fundamental articles, viz., reverence for the deity—abstaining from evil—and behaving valiantly in battle; and the triad rule for the preservation of health was—cheerfulness—temperance—exercise.[1] Indeed, the number three was sacred throughout all antiquity.[2] And both Aristotle and Plutarch could say, equally with the British Druids, that it was held mysterious, because it comprehended the

---

[1] Smith, Gael. Ant., p. 80.
[2] Virg. Ecl., viii. 78. Plato in Tim. Plut. de Isid. et Osir., p. 373. Ovid, vii. 189. Olaus Mag. Hist. Goth. Asiat. Res., vol. i. p. 272, vol. iii. p. 359, &c. &c.

beginning—middle—end. The jovial Horace also exclaims:—

> Tribus aut novem
> Miscentur cyathis pocula commodis.
> Qui musas amat impares,
> Ternos ter cyathos attonitus petet
> Vates; tres prohibet supra
> Rixarum metuens tangere Gratia
> Nudis juncta sororibus.[1]

Very superstitious ideas were attached to bells in the first ages of Christianity; and the opposition to the Pelagian heresy, and the Druidical triads united, probably produced that singular exhibition of veneration for the Trinity which is thus recorded. Three clergymen of St Telian's three churches claimed his body when dead; upon which three several corpses appeared, and one was buried in each of these churches. And Giraldus Cambrensis records, that three persons usually sat down to the table in honour of the Trinity at the period when he flourished.[2] Nor are the superstitions attached to this number yet extinguished. Scheffer tells us that the Laplanders are in the habit of using a cord tied with three magical knots for raising the wind. When they untie the first knot, there blows a favourable gale of wind; which increases at the second, and becomes a perfect hurricane at the third. Most of the northern nations were addicted to this superstition. Amongst the Mandingoes, in the interior of Africa, according to Park, when a child is

[1] Hor., l. iii. carm. 19. [2] Fosbr. Monach., p. 16.

named, the priest, after the blessing, whispers something into the child's ear, and spits three times in his face, after which the name is pronounced, and the child placed in its mother's arms.[1]

To come a little nearer home. Martin, in his book on the Isles of Scotland, gives several instances of the superstitious use of the above number. "When the inhabitants," he says, "go a-fowling, in order to prevent the transgression of the least nicety, every novice is always joined with another, who can instruct him in all the punctilios observed on such occasions. When arrived at their destination, after uncovering their heads, turning round sun-ways, and thanking God, they pray three times in three different places; the first prayer is made as they approach the chapel; the second in going round it, and the third in the interior." Even some of our learned Freemasons did not escape the taint of these superstitious observances. Our learned brother Elias Ashmole, when he had the ague, used to take a good dose of elixir early in the morning, and to hang about his neck three spiders; and this, he says, drove the ague away.[2] In the "Life of a Satirical Puppy,"[3] the following passage occurs: "One of his guardians, being fortified with an old charm, marches cross-legged, spitting three times, east, west, and south; and afterwards

---

[1] Brand and Sir Henry Ellis, in the Popular Antiquities, have collected many curious facts respecting the number three.
[2] Diary, 11th April 1681.   [3] Lond. 1657, p. 35.

prefers his vallor to a catechising office. In the name of God, quoth he, what art thou? whence dost thou come? seeing something that he supposed to be a ghost."

What a weak and unstable creature is man! We all despise these idle fancies in others, and yet, I am persuaded, there is scarcely an individual at present in existence, notwithstanding the improvements in science and philosophy which distinguish our own times, who is not, in some respect or other, under their influence. Is there no young lady amongst us who will sit cross-legged at the card-table as the harbinger of good-luck? Is no one alarmed at hearing the death-watch, or the sight of a single magpie crossing his path? I knew a man—an educated man too—who always removed his hat on such an occurrence. Which of us is really and truly exempt from the dread of apparitions and visions of the night; or from a belief in the efficacy of charms for ague, cramp, or toothache? Let every one answer to himself, and not to the world, and his reply will be not far from the truth.

Again. What opinion shall we pass upon the pseudo-prophecies of Francis Moore, physician, and his imitators, who have assumed the cabalistic names of Raphael, Zadkiel, &c.? Of what value would their predictions be if their authors did not place a greater dependence on the credulity of mankind than on the stars and planets? Such men fatten upon the weaknesses of their fellow-creatures, and turn their superstitious feelings to account. Southey, speaking of John Müller, better known under the name of Regiomontanus, says, "He could talk of the fiery and earthy trigons, the aerial and the watery, and of that property of a triangle whereby Sol and Jupiter, Luna and Venus, Saturn and Mercury, respectively become joint trigonocrators, leaving Mars to rule over the watery trigon alone." This is the kind of jargon which won golden opinions from all sorts of men a century or two back. It not only advanced the science of astrology to eminence, but excited such a general belief in the art of transmuting metals, that an alarm was taken in the highest quarters, and an Act of Parliament was passed, 5 Henry IV., 1404, determining that "the making of gold and silver shall be deemed felony." "This law," says Watson,[1] "is said to have resulted from the fear at that time entertained by the Lords and Commons, lest the executive power, finding itself by these means enabled to increase the revenue of the Crown to any degree it pleased, should disdain to ask aid from the Legislature; and in consequence should degenerate into tyranny and arbitrary power."

The use of the number three is so firmly incorporated into many of our civil and religious ceremonies, that its observance has become an immovable item in the habits and customs of the people. Thus public approbation of a toast or sentiment is displayed at a banquet by the honours of three or three times three acclama-

[1] Chemical Essays, vol. i.

tions. When a hostile British man-of-war meets the enemy, the seamen salute him with three hearty cheers. And the passing bell, at the decease of any individual, commences and concludes with three distinct knells for a man, and two for a woman, each repeated three times for the following reason, as is recorded in an old English homily for Trinity Sunday: "The fourme of the Trinity was founden in manne, that was Adam our forefadir, of earth oon personne, and Eve of Adam the secunde persone; and of them both was the third persone. At the deth of a manne three bellis shulde be ronge, as his knyll, in worscheppe of the Trinetee, and for a womanne, who was the secunde persone of the Trinetee, two bellis should be rungen."[1] In a word, not only in reference to the Trinity, and to the death and resurrection of Christ at three days' distance from each other, but from many ancient superstitions both Jewish and heathen, the number three is likely to retain the reputation of possessing mysterious properties as long as man shall remain upon the earth.

In attempting to explain the arcane peculiarities of the number three we might be accused of travelling out of the record. But there will be no impropriety in remarking that numbers which increase in arithmetical progression by threes, the sum of the first and last terms will be equal to that of the second and last but one, or the two middle terms, if two, or twice the middle one if an unit. Thus, for instance, if we take a progres-

[1] See Strutt's Manners and Customs, vol. iii. p. 176.

sion by threes consisting of six terms, it will stand as follows, viz., 1, 4, 7, 10, 13, 16. And $16+1=17$; $4+13=17$; $10+7=17$. Again, in 7 terms, viz., 1, 4, 7, 10, 13, 16, 19, the same peculiarity occurs, as $1+19=20$; $4+16=20$, &c., and twice $10=20$. And here the seventh term is equal to the first with the addition of 6 times 3, as $1+18=19$.

PROGRESSIVE GENERATION OF THE TETRAD OR SOLID, REPRESENTING FIRE.

THE SOLID, TETRAD, QUATERNARY, OR THE NUMBER FOUR.

CHAPTER IV.

THE SOLID.

TETRAD, QUATERNARY, OR THE NUMBER FOUR.

"By that pure, holy, Four-Letter NAME on high,
Nature's eternal fountain and supply,
The parent of all souls that living be,
By Him, with faithful oath, I swear to thee."
OATH OF PYTHAGORAS.

"THE Grand and Sacred Name ought to be saluted four times in four peculiar positions, for the following reasons."—OLD LECTURES.

THE tetrad, though not essentially masonic, for the only instances in which it is exemplified, viz., in the Sacred Name and the Cherubim, are attached to the *third* degree only, was esteemed the most perfect number, and referred to the Author of nature, or T.G.A.O.T.U.; and his name was therefore composed of four letters, יהוה, and was called Tetragrammaton by the Jews, and Tetractys by the Gentiles; of the latter of whom Hierocles, in his exposition of the Golden Verses of Pythagoras, says, "He is the Demiurgus, the architect and maker of all things." These are his words: "The author of these verses shows that the tetrad, which is the fountain of the perpetual orderly distribution of things, is the same with God who is the Demiurgus; an intelligible god, the source of the celestial and sensible good." The tetrad, as Mr Taylor thinks, is, however, the *animal itself* of Plato, who, as Syrianus justly observes, was the best of the Pythagoreans; subsists at the extremity of the intelligible triad, as is most satisfactorily shown by Proclus in the third book of his treatise on the theology of Plato. And between these two triads, the one intelligible, and the other intellectual, another order of gods exists, which partakes of both extremes.

This number forms the arithmetical mean between the monad and the heptad; and this comprehends all powers, both of the productive and produced numbers; for this, of all numbers under ten, is made of a certain number; the duad doubled makes a tetrad, and the tetrad doubled makes the hebdomad. Two multiplied into itself produces four; and retorted into itself makes the first cube. This first cube is a fertile number, the ground of multitude and variety, constituted of two and four. Thus the two principles of temporal things, the pyramis and cube, form and matter, flow from one fountain, the tetragon, whose idea is the Tetractys, the divine exemplar.[1]

Amongst the Hermesians, the number four, thus

---

[1] Reuchlin è Cabala, l. ii.

amplified into a cube, was the symbol of truth, because in whatever point of view it may be contemplated it is always the same; and for this reason Hermes or Mercury was esteemed the god of eloquence;[1] and the Greeks and Romans offered to him in sacrifice the tongues of animals. The gift of eloquence, however, according to Lucian, was conferred by the Druids of Britain on a different deity. He was told by one of the Druids, as he stood admiring a figure of Hercules, to whose tongue were fastened chains of gold and amber, which drew along a multitude of persons whose ears appeared to be fixed to the other end of those chains, that "they did not agree with the Greeks in making Mercury the god of eloquence. According to our system," he continued, "this honour is due only to Hercules, because he surpasses Mercury in power; we paint him advanced in age, because eloquence does not exert her most animated powers except in the mouths of aged persons. The link, and the connection there is between the tongue of the eloquent and the ears of the audience, justify the rest of the representation. By understanding the history of Hercules in this sense, we neither dishonour him nor depart from truth; for we hold it indisputably true that he succeeded in all his noble enterprises, captivated every heart, and subdued every brutal passion, not by the strength of his arms, but by the power of wisdom and the sweetness of his persuasion."

[1] Tertul. de coronis Festus.

The most ancient Greeks[1] considered the tetrad to be the root and principle of all things, because it was the number of the elements. The *fire* was considered to be Jupiter, the *air* Juno, the *earth* Pluto, and *water*, taken from the womb, Nestis. On this subject Pythagoras taught that when fire resolves the dissolution of water into air, two parts of air are generated, and one part of fire. But when, on the contrary, water is generated from air, three parts of air being resolved, the four triangles which are mingled together from the same cause, *i.e.*, from condensation, together with two parts of air, make one part of water.

In the system of the Rose +, as propounded by Fludd, Behmen, Meyer, and others, the four elements were represented as being peopled and governed by spirits, who possessed a decided influence over the destiny of man. These elementary beings, which to grosser eyes were invisible, were familiarly known to the initiated. To be admitted to their acquaintance, it was previously necessary that the organs of human sight should be purged by the universal medicine, and that certain glass globes should be chemically prepared with one or other of the four elements, and for one month exposed to the beams of the sun. These preliminary steps being taken, the initiated immediately had a sight of innumerable beings of a luminous substance, but of thin and evanescent structure, that people the elements on all sides of us. Those who

[1] See Plut. de Plac. Phil., p. 878.

inhabited the air were called sylphs; and those who dwelt in the earth bore the name of gnomes; such as peopled the fire were salamanders; and those who made their home in the waters were called undines. Each class appears to have had an extensive power in the element to which it belonged. They could raise tempests in the air, and storms at sea, shake the earth, and alarm the inhabitants of the globe with the sight of devouring flames. They were, however, more formidable in appearance than in reality. And the whole race was subordinate to man, and particularly subject to the initiated. The gnomes, inhabitants of the earth and the mines, liberally supplied to the human beings with whom they conversed the hidden treasures over which they presided. The four classes were some of them male, and some female; but the female sex seems to have preponderated."[1] Thus Pope :—

> For when the fair in all their pride expire,
> To their first elements their souls retire,
> The sprites of fiery termagants in flame
> Mount up, and take a Salamander's name.
> Soft yielding minds to water glide away,
> And sip, with Nymphs, their elemental tea.
> The graver prude sinks downward to a Gnome,
> In search of mischief still on earth to roam.
> The light coquettes in Sylphs aloft repair,
> And sport and flutter in the fields of air.[2]

The figure of a cross, to symbolise the four elements, formed a disquisition in one of the Theo-

---

[1] Godwin's Lives of Necromancers, p. 36.
[2] Rape of the Lock, Canto i. 57.

sophic degrees of M. Peuvret, called the Rosy Cross; and was treated according to the fundamental principles of light and darkness, or good and evil. Thus the element of air corresponded with humility in the former class, and pride in the latter. The earth, in like manner, was assimilated with meekness on the one hand and covetousness on the other; water with patience and envy; and fire with love and hatred. These principles, arising out of the world's four elements, when applied to the science of light, were denominated the four elements of God, and to darkness, the four elements of the devil. The philosophy of the subject was thus stated · "The fire preys upon the water and air; the air is breathed out of the water by the incitement of the fire; the water is the contraction of the air by the vicinity of the astringent cold earth, but the earth is one body of no great intimacy with either of the other, being only a sediment resulting from the separating power of the other three elements. Nor yet may it be wondered that the four were once one, and proceeded from one; seeing they are still one, differing only in the degrees of rarity and density; for as the earth drives up the water, so doth the water raise up the air, and the fire being violently active surmounts all." The lecture then goes on to explain how the one was separated into four; but the exposition is too long and too dry to be inserted here.

It should appear that the aboriginal savages of America (if savages they were) had some attachment to the number four; for the Mexican priests were enjoined to burn incense before the image of the deity four times a day. They had a public celebration or general jubilee every four years; and forty days before the annual festival of Quetzalcoatl, the Mexican Mercury, a slave was purchased, and fattened as a victim to be sacrificed at the solemnity; while the lives of four children were offered to Tlaloc, the god of rain, when the corn was bursting into spike, in order that he might be propitious, and by sending genial showers, produce a good and plentiful harvest.

These sacrifices were offered on the summit of four square pyramids constructed for the purpose; some of which remain in Central America to the present day; and one of them is thus described by Stephens [1] "It is sixty feet high, and one hundred feet square at the base; but it is now covered with earth, and though it retains the symmetry of its original proportions, it is so overgrown with trees, that it appears a mere wooded hill, but peculiar in its regularity of shape. *Four* grand staircases, each twenty-five feet wide, ascended to an esplanade within six feet of the top. This esplanade was six feet in width, and on each side is a smaller staircase leading to the top. The summit is a plain stone platform, fifteen feet square. Probably it was the great mound of sacrifice, on which the priests, in the sight of the assembled people,

[1] Travels in Yucatan, vol. i. p. 131.

cut out the hearts of human victims. At a short distance from the base of the mound was an opening in the earth, forming another of those extraordinary caves which have been already mentioned. The entrance was by a broken, yawning mouth, steep, and requiring some care in the descent. At the first resting-place, the mouth opened into an extensive subterraneous chamber with a high roof, and passages branching off in every direction. In different places were remains of fires and the bones of animals, showing that it had probably been a place of refuge, or residence of men; and in the entrance of one of these passages we found a sculptured idol."[1]

In Geometry, the tetrad combines within itself all the materials of which the world and all things therein are composed, viz., the point extended to a line; a line to a superficies; and the superficies or triad converted to a solid or tetrad by the point being placed over it. Thus in the original lectures of Masonry, which, like those of the Druids, were constructed rhythmically, that they might be more easily remembered, we have the following passage:—

> The Science five [Geometry] may well compose
> A noble structure, vast;
> A point, a line, a superfice,
> But solid is the last.

According to Philo Judæus, the quadrate

---

[1] See Hist. Init., p. 294, new ed., where the use of these caverns is particularly described.

number not only comprehends all, point, line, superficies, and body, but possesses other perfections, one of which is, that all the first numbers of which it is formed make up the number TEN, which is so perfect, that in counting we can go no farther; for the parts of four added together, as $1+2+3+4=10$. But Hierocles the Pythagorean contends that before we make up ten by this process, we must consider that there is an implicit and complicate entireness of *ten* in the number *four*, which is of itself amply sufficient to constitute it a symbol of universality.

Another excellence is also found in the number four, viz., that the principal consonances of music, which are the diapente, diatessaron, and diapason, are found to contain the same parts of this number. The diapente, which is the sesquialtera, as from 9 to 6; the diatessaron is a sesquitertia, as from 8 to 6; and the diapason, which is a double, as 12 to 6. The quadrate number was highly appreciated by the ancients on account of the four liberal arts—Geometry, Astronomy, Music, and Arithmetic, which are highly important in the acquirement of all other sciences.[1]

From the above reasoning, the tetrad or tetractys was called *Kosmos*, the world, because it numbered 36, the sum of the four odd numbers 1, 3, 5, 7, proceeding from a combination of the digits, thus:—

[1] Concil., vol. i. p. 106.

$$1 + 2 = 3$$
$$3 + 4 = 7$$
$$5 + 6 = 11$$
$$7 + 8 = 15$$
$$\overline{36}$$

The Pythagorean world, according to Plutarch,[1] consisted of a double quaternary. The quaternary of the intellectual world is T'Agathon, Nous, Psyche, Hyle; while that of the sensible world, which is properly what Pythagoras meant by the word Kosmos, is Fire, Air, Water, and Earth. The four elements are called by the name of *rizomata*, the roots or principles of all mixed bodies. In some ancient Greek verses to this effect, Jupiter is the fire, Juno the air, Pluto the earth, and Nestis the water, and these are the four roots of all existing things.

"The intelligible world proceeds out of the divine mind after this manner. The Tetractys, reflecting upon its own essence, the first unit, productrix of all things, and on its own beginning, saith thus: Once one, twice two, immediately ariseth a tetrad, having on its top the highest unit, and *becomes a Pyramis*, whose base is a plain tetrad, answerable to a superficies, upon which the radiant light of the divine unity produceth the form of incorporeal fire, by reason of the descent of Juno (matter) to inferior things. Hence ariseth essential light, not burning but illuminating. This is the creation of the middle

[1] De anim. procr., 1027.

world, which the Hebrews call the Supreme, the world of the deity. It is termed Olympus, entirely light, and replete with separate forms, where is the seat of the immortal gods, *deum domus alta*, whose top is unity, its wall trinity, and its superficies quaternity."[1]

It forms a curious coincidence with this philosophy, that the Arabian analysis of female beauty should be founded on the same principles, and thus made to consist of $4 \times 9 = 36$ excellences. "Four things in a woman," says an anonymous author quoted by Lane,[2] "should be black: the hair of her head, the eyebrows, the eyelashes, and the dark part of the eyes;—four white: the complexion of the skin, the white of the eyes, the teeth, and the legs;—four red: the tongue, the lips, the middle of the cheeks, and the gums;—four round: the head, the neck, the forearms, and the ankles;—four long: the back, the fingers, the arms, and the legs;—four wide: the forehead, the eyes, the bosom, and the hips;—four fine: the eyebrows, the nose, the lips, and the fingers;—four thick: the lower part of the back, the thighs, the calves of the legs, and the knees;—four small: the ears, the breasts, the hands, and the feet;—in all, thirty-six."

The number four had a very significant reference to masculine or manly performances; and to body and soul, because it consists of four properties, mind, science, opinion, and sense;[3] and also to

---

[1] Reuchlin, *ut supra*, p. 689.   [2] Arabian Nights, vol. i. p. 29.
[3] Plut. Plac. Phil., i. 3.

justice, because being quadrate, it is divided into equals, and is itself equal.[1] It was a symbol of Wisdom. Pierius says,[2] "Sapientiam in quadrato statuebant; ex hoc hieroglyphico volubilem illam, uti paulo ante diximus, hujus verò sedem firmam et inconcussam indicantes. Et nostri quadrata ligna quæ ad arcæ Noes fabricam parari divinum jussit numen, doctores et magistros in Ecclesia significare dicunt, quorum sapientia inclusi intus populi conservantur, et ab incursantibus hæreticorum procellis muniuntur. Ex quadratis enin lignis construere debere nos Bibliothecam admonet Admantius, non ex agrestibus, rudibus, et impolitis. Quippe ex Propheticis et Apostolicis voluminibus, in quivus solis vera continentur sapientia, utpote qui vitiis omnibus resectis excisisque, quadratum vitæ justioris tenorem."

The name of Harmony was given to the tetrad, because it is a diatessaron in sesquitertia. The Pythagoreans, however, were of opinion, according to Theon in his "Mathematica," that the division of the canon of the monochord was made by the tetractys in the duad, triad, and tetrad; for it comprehends a sesquitertia, a sesquialtera, a duple, a triple, and a quadruple proportion, the section of which is 27. In the ancient musical notation, the tetrachord consisted of three degrees or intervals, and four terms or sounds, called by the Greeks diatessaron and by us a fourth. In the ancient music, all the primitive or chief divisions were confined to four chords, so that the great

[1] Alex. Aphrod. metath., v.   [2] Hieroglyphica, fo. 290.

scale consisted of replicates, and all the upper tetrachords were considered only as repetitions of the first and lowest, called Hypate Hypaton; the third sound of which, answering to our D natural on the third line of the bass, was called Hypate diatonus; while the Hypate meson was the principal of the mean tetrachord, and equivalent to our E natural on the third space in the bass.

The same number was called by the Pythagoreans the key-keeper of nature, because the constitution of the world cannot exist without it; and the square or cube being equivalent to truth is considered equally applicable to nature. It was denominated also Hercules, Impetuosity, Strongest, Masculine, Ineffeminate, Mercury, Vulcan, Bacchus, Soritas, Maiades, Erynnis, Socus, Dioscorus, Bassarius, Two-Mothered, of Feminine Form, of Virile Performance, Bacchation, with a variety of other names.[1] The Talmudists say that four things are able to annul an evil decree against any person, how guilty soever he may be, which are Charity, Acquittal, Change of Name, and Change of Conduct. From this belief some of them superstitiously think that this tetrad will cure the most severe sickness. And the number four includes the winding up and result of every man's probation; for all things will terminate in death, judgment, heaven, and hell. To avoid the latter of which St Irenæus says, that "four gospels were given, and no more, from the four winds and four corners of the earth."

[1] Stanley, Pyth., p. 61.

A curious argument has been used by St Augustine to prove that Christ could not possibly have added to the number of His apostles, which is derived from the tetrad before us; he says, "The gospel was to be preached *in the four corners of the earth in the name of the Trinity,* and three times four make twelve"! A modern sect of Christians, perhaps in imitation of this and the like mode of reasoning, assumed the name of Mystics, and contended for the propriety of allegorising Scripture by a quadruple process. For instance, they put this construction upon the city of Jerusalem. *Literally,* they said, it is a city of Judea; if understood *allegorically,* it is the Church militant; if *morally,* a sincere Christian; and if *mystically,* heaven, the Church triumphant.

The Tetragrammaton, or four-lettered NAME of the Most High, יהוה, appears to have been known to the heathen. Archbishop Tenison says,[1] "This Name was no mystery among the Greeks, as is evident from the mention of Jerombaal, a priest of the god Ieuo, in Sanchoniathon; of Jaho in St Hierom, and the Sibylline Oracles; of Jaoth, or Jaho in Irenæus; of the Hebrew God called Jaoia by the Gnostics; of Jaou in Clemens Alexandrinus; of Jao, the first principle of the first Gnostic heaven in Epiphanius; the God of Moses in Diodorus Siculus; the god Bacchus in the oracle of Apollo Clarius; and lastly, as was said, of the Samaritan god Jabe, in Theodoret."

This Name is called by Josephus "the Sacred

[1] Idolat., p. 404.

Letters—the shuddering Name of God;" and Caligula, in Philo, swears to him and the ambassadors, by the God with the unpronounceable Name. The Tetragrammaton, even down to the seventeenth century of Christianity, was esteemed a powerful amulet. Thus Stephens, speaking of a witch, says, " Her prayers and Amen be a charm and a curse; her contemplations and soule's delight bee other men's mischiefe; her portion and sutors be her soule and a succubus; her highest adorations be yew-trees, dampish churchyards, and a fayre moonlight; *her best preservatives be odde numbers and mightie Tetragrammaton."*[1]

It was a doctrine taught by the Hebrew philosophers that "the Tetragrammaton and אתיה alike represent the substance of the Divinity; the latter being in the future tense and first person singular, and the Tetragrammaton in the third person, forming, between the two, these three words, תית תוה אהיה Was, Is, Will be. R. Judah à Levi in the Cuzari, and the learned Aben Ezra, on the 33d chapter of Exodus, also explain that the name יה is likewise the substance; for the Tetragrammaton is numerically 26, and the two letters יה, written at full length יור תא, are also 26. And this is what the Lord said to Moses, 'Say unto Israel, The Tetragrammaton and אתית hath sent me unto you;' for, on his inquiry what he should say if they asked him the Name of the divine Essence, He answered the two names it signifies. Some learned Jews understand the

[1] Characters, p. 375.

words, What is His name? to mean, What is His Being or Essence?"[1]

Marcellus Ficin observes on Plato, as we are told by the Rabbi ben Israel, that the Name of the Lord is written and pronounced by all nations with *four* letters. The Egyptians called Him *Teut;* the Arabs, *Alla;* the Persians, *Sire;* the Magi, *Orsi;* the Mahometans, *Abdi;* the Greeks, *Teos;* the ancient Turks, *Esar;* and the Latins, *Deus;* to which John Lorenzo Anania adds, the Germans call him *Gott;* the Surmatas, *Bouh* and *Istu;* the Tartars, *Itga.*

In the Continental degree, called the Philosophes Inconnus, the number four is thus noticed: "Que signifie le nombre *Quatre* adopté dans le Grand Ecossisme de S. André d'Ecosse, le complement des progressions maçonniques? Outre le parfait équilibre et le parfait égalité des quatre élémens dans le pierre physique, il signifie quatre choses qu'il faut faire nécessairement pour l'accomplissement de l'œuvre, qui sont, *composition, alteration, mixtion, et union,* lesquelles, une fois faites dans les règles de l'art, donneront les fils légitimes du soleil, et produiront le phénix toujours renaissant de ses cendres."

There is a curious anecdote told respecting this number, of Pope Innocent III., who sent to our King John a present of four rings set with four different-coloured jewels; admonishing him at the same time to consider seriously their four

[1] Concil., vol. i. p. 107.

various properties of form, number, matter, and colour. The form, being round, shadowed out eternity, for which it was his duty to prepare; the number denoted the four cardinal virtues, which it was his duty to practise; the matter, being gold, the most precious of metals, designated wisdom, the most precious of accomplishments, which it was his duty to acquire; and as to the colour, the green of the emerald represented faith; the blue of the sapphire, hope; the redness of the ruby, charity; and the splendid yellow of the topaz, good works."[1]

The preceding observations on the philosophy of the number four, will be received by the fraternity, not as a perfect essay on the subject, but as a series of collections towards such a dissertation; which, if it were to be fully developed and exemplified, would far exceed my limits. In 1636, Beeton published a book on "The Figure of Foore," which I notice simply as a curious repository of ingenious conjecture, although it contains nothing to our purpose, being constructed on the plan of the subjoined specimen. "There are foure great cyphers in the world, hee that is lame among dauncers, dumbe among lawyers, dull among schollers, and rude among courtiers. Again—there are foure things grievously empty: a head without braines, a wit without judgment, a heart without honesty, and a purse without money."

If brevity be the soul of wit, it is also a bar to the exercise of judgment, or the play of imagina-

[1] Beckmann, Ancient Inventions, vol. ii. p. 171.

tion. A few dry facts strung together are not favourable to the *currente calamo*, or pen of the ready writer. If, however, there is no theory to establish, or system to demonstrate, the writer will escape the chances of offering contradictory arguments, or of urging opinions which are at variance with fact. This is something; and may serve as a set-off against the charge of dulness and ultra-gravity, even where gravity is most appositely used—in a dissertation on the subject of Freemasonry. Now, as the composition of a delicious beverage may be considered by some of our brethren as connected, in a slight degree, with the refreshments of the Lodge, I shall attempt to relieve the dulness of these dissertations by transcribing the opinion of a philosopher who illuminates the pages of *Blackwood's Magazine*, on the ingredients of a liquor called punch, as it is in some measure illustrative of the number under our consideration. He pronounces, *ex cathedra*, that it ought, like the fourth interval in music, to be founded on the principles of the tetrad. These are his words: "Punch is a liquor made by mixing spirit and water, sugar and the juice of lemon, and formerly with spice; and is so called from an Indian wood called five, that being the number of the ingredients. The Greek equivalent for punch, or more properly poünch, is διὰ πεντε; but the spice is now admissible only in *bishop:* wherefore in the universities, and in convocations of the clergy, and in other assemblies of learned men, punch is more correctly called διὰ τεσσαρων, signifying *a combination of four.*" A small modicum of the latter composition is not to be despised, particularly if the three weaker ingredients be well amalgamated and smoking hot, before it is enlivened by the spirit. Can I conclude this chapter more *sweetly?* It is very doubtful; and therefore I shall leave it unattempted.

GEOMETRICAL APPLICATION OF THE PENTAD OR PYRAMID, REPRESENTING WATER.

THE PYRAMID, PENTAD, QUINCUNX, OR THE NUMBER FIVE.

CHAPTER V.

THE PYRAMID.

PENTAD, QUINCUNX, OR THE NUMBER FIVE.

"The Blazing Star is depicted with five points or rays, to show, first, that in the construction of the Temple, five orders of architecture were made use of ; secondly, to represent the five points of felicity ; *i.e.*, to walk, to intercede for, to pray, to love, and to assist your brethren, so as to be united with them right heartily; thirdly, to represent the five senses, which constitute the dignity of man ; fourthly, to symbolise the five lights of Masonry ; and fifthly, the five zones inhabited by the fraternity."—The Ineffable Lectures.

IT is remarkable that every number presents some charm, which may be applied to a purpose not only peculiar to itself, but also not transferable to any other subject without impairing its efficiency. So thought our forefathers; and the question is, Do not we think the same ? I have already mentioned our predilection for the number three, and three times three cheers ; would five, or five times five, answer the same purpose ? It is not to be thought of. There is not an assemblage of Englishmen, from the highest to the lowest rank, but would resist the innovation. If any one be troubled with that unsightly excrescence in the eye, which is called in some provinces a *stye,* it can only be cured by drawing a lady's wedding-ring nine times across the diseased part—no other number would do. The charm would be profitless if it were exceeded or diminished by a single unit. The number thirteen is supposed to be unpropitious at a dinner-party—one of the company is expected to die within the year; but no such belief is attached to twelve or fourteen, or any larger or smaller number.

Again, the seventh son of a seventh son, no daughter intervening, is considered to be a physician by birth, and to be intuitively imbued with a knowledge of the symptoms and treatment of diseases; but no such superstitious belief is attached to any other son, who has hence no source of knowledge but what arises from incessant and severe study. In an old Book of Knowledge, the following paragraph occurs: " Astronomers and astrologers say that in the beginning of March, the seventh night, or the fourteenth day, let thee bloud of the right arm; and in the beginning of April, the eleventh day, of the left arm; and in the end of May, third or fifth day, on whether arm thou wilt; and thus, of all that year, thou shalt orderly be kept from the fever, the falling gout, the sister gout, and losse of thy sight." About the middle of the last century, or a little later, there lived a curious character, well known by the appellation of King Cole. He was a fish salesman at Billingsgate, and on the day of the liberation of the celebrated John Wilkes, he always invited 45 friends to dine; and he treated them with a plum-pudding containing 45 pounds of flour and 45 of fruit. It was boiled 45 hours, and conveyed to the place, where the party were at dinner, with flags and music, and 45 butchers with marrow-bones and cleavers. There were also upon the table 45 pigeon-pies and 45 apple-dumplings. When this old man lost his son he consoled himself by using the same mystical number. He had him buried 45 miles from town, attended by 45 fishmongers; he paid the sexton 45 shillings for 45 tolls of the bell; and mourned 45 days in deep, and 45 days in half mourning.

How is this attachment to certain numbers to be accounted for? Let the physiologist find it out if he can; if not, let him go to the Delphic oracle, for I have no time for speculations on such a mysterious subject. In the case of the old fishmonger, however, the solution is easy. In most other cases, if there were any truth in the facts—which we are sure there is not—all that could be said about the matter would be, that as they were contrary to any demonstrable principle of science or philosophy, they would constitute so many vagaries of Nature, departing from her staid and sober march, to display a series of hallucinations which derogate from her dignity of demeanour, as exceptions to her unerring rules.

The belief in the efficacy of particular numbers is too firmly fixed in the mind to admit of being extinguished by the arguments of sober reason, be they ever so specious and sound. It extends through all ranks of society, and travels side by side with other superstitions, the existence of which is a libel on the reason and understanding of man. It preys upon his spirits, forces his inclinations out of their proper bias, compels him to believe what, in his inward conscience, he suspects to be delusive; and induces his fears to admit what his judgment pronounces to be false.

It is a curious fact, that though we affect to pity the ignorance of those rude barbarians of antiquity, who could believe that when the sun and moon disappeared beneath the horizon, they became impure spirits, and wandered about the world till break of day; yet we admit, at least inwardly, the doctrine of wraiths, ghosts, apparitions, and perhaps fairies; and fancy that departed spirits or fiends linger over a forgotten hoard of gold till it be appropriated to the lawful owner. Sir Walter Scott has accorded an illustration of this kind of superstition, which was furnished by his friend James Skene, Esq.[1] "Near the little village of Franchemont, near Spaw, stands an ancient castle, which is the subject of many superstitious legends. It is firmly believed by the neighbouring peasantry, that the last baron deposited in one of the vaults of the castle a ponderous chest, containing an immense treasure in gold and silver, which by some magic spell was

[1] Marmion, canto vi. note 7.

intrusted to the care of the devil, who constantly sits on the chest in the shape of a huntsman. Any one who is adventurous enough to touch the chest is instantly seized with the palsy. On a certain occasion, a priest of noted piety was brought to the vault, who used all the arts of exorcism to persuade his infernal majesty to vacate his seat, but in vain; for the huntsman remained immovable. At last, moved by the earnestness of the priest, he told him that he would agree to resign the chest if he would sign his name with blood. But the priest understood his meaning, and refused, as by that act he would have delivered over his soul to the devil. Yet it is still believed, that if any one should discover the mystical words used by the person who deposited the treasure, and pronounce them over the chest, the fiend would instantly decamp."

The reality of this superstition is undoubted; and it was so prevalent during the eighteenth century, that directions were formally given to regulate the conduct of a discovery of such a secret hoard, by a German writer of the name of Stryck. He says, "If the spirit stands by and remains neuter, have nothing to do with the treasure; it is a temptation from Satan to burn your fingers—there let it lie. But if the spectre offers it, and presses it upon you, you may take it safely."

These superstitions are partly the effect of some undefined principle in our nature, which suggests, we know not how, that there are beings superior to ourselves, by whom our actions are governed and directed; and under this impression we submit to unforeseen calamities, without using any means to prevent their approach. The superstitionist, as Plutarch says when speaking on this subject, "accounts every little distemper in his body, or decay in his estate, the death of his children, or other crosses or disappointments, as the immediate effects of God's anger, and the incursions of some vindictive demon. And therefore he never attempts to use any remedy for his relief, lest he should seem to fight against God, or despise His correction." Amongst Christians, however, this feeling of despair ought never to be indulged, because it has been revealed to us that the prayer of a broken and a contrite heart will neither be despised nor overlooked by a gracious God, who willeth not the death of a sinner, but had much rather he would repent and be saved. The feeling, however, remains unsubdued at the present day; and, strange to tell, neither reason nor revelation have been able to neutralise its influence over the human mind.

The pentad is a primary number, because it is divisible by unity only. *It is the Pyramis itself;* "the species of fire, of which a Pyramis, having four bases and equal angles, is compounded, the most immovable and penetrant form, without matter, essential, separate light, next to God sempiternal life. The work of the mind is life; the work of God is immortality—eternal life. God himself is not this created Light, but the author of it, whereof in the divine Trinity He containeth a most absolute pyramid, which implieth the vigour of fire; and is formed of the tetrad with a point over the centre joined by right lines to each angle; and thus forming the pentad; but the pyramid is the fiery light of the material world, of separate intelligences, beyond the visible heaven, termed age, eternity, ether; which, being placed, like the uppermost point of the pyramid, high above the tetrad, is free from any disturbance by the other four."[1]

This number completes both odd and even; and hence refers to Geometry, which, according to an ancient masonic arrangement, is the fifth science, and was thus expressed in the old lectures:—

> By letters four, and Science five,
> This Ⓖ aright doth stand
> In art and due proportion.
> You have your answer, friend.

And hence we refer the number five that are competent to hold a Fellow Craft's Lodge, to the five senses, the five orders of architecture, and the five points of fellowship. In Geometry, however, the pentad is more particularly represented by the five regular bodies; which, on account of their singularity, and the mysterious nature usually ascribed to them, were formerly known by the name of "the five Platonic bodies." The ancients regarded them with so much veneration, that it is said our Grand Master Euclid composed his Elements for the express purpose of illustrating their

---

[1] Reuchlin, *ut supra*, p. 68?.

peculiar properties. These five bodies were called —1, the tetraedon, which has four equal triangular faces; 2, the hexaedron, or cube, which has six equal square faces; 3, the octaedron, which has eight equal triangular faces; 4, the dodecaedron, which has twelve equal pentagonal faces; and 5, the icosaedron, which has twenty equal triangular faces. These are the only forms which it is possible for regular bodies to assume. Kepler was transported with joy when he made a discovery which he conceived to be founded on these principles. He exclaimed in rapture: "What I prophesied two-and-twenty years ago, as soon as I discovered the five solids among the heavenly orbits,—what I firmly believed long before I had seen Ptolemy's Harmonics,—what I had promised to my friends in the title of this book, which I named before I was sure of my discovery,—what sixteen years ago I urged as a thing to be sought, —that for which I joined Tycho Brahe and settled in Prague,—for which I have devoted the best part of my life to astronomical contemplations; at length I have brought to light, and have recognised its truth beyond my most sanguine expectations!"

And what does the reader think the profound discovery was which thus excited this great astronomer? Why, it was—that as nature had produced only five regular bodies, there could not possibly be more than six planets attached to our system! And his theory was thus enunciated: "It so happens that there are only five regular solids, *i.e.*, it is possible to make only five solids of different numbers of faces, so that all the faces of each solid shall be equal to each other; viz., the tetraedron; the cube, or hexaedron; the solid of eight faces, or the octaedron; the solid of twelve faces, or the dodecaedron; and the solid of twenty faces, or the icosaedron. The orbit of the earth is the ruler of all. Place within this orbit, touching it at all points, an icosaedron, and draw within it a circle that will touch all its faces internally, and we have the orbit of Venus. Within the orbit of Venus place an octaedron, and draw a circle as before—that is the orbit of Mercury. Outside the orbit of the earth, place a dodecaedron, and around this solid draw a circle, which is the orbit of Mars. Outside of the orbit of Mars describe a tetraedron, and around this draw a circle, and you will have the orbit of Jupiter; and if you describe a hexaedron outside of this orbit, you will have that of Saturn. Now there are no more regular bodies, therefore there can be no more planets; and the observed distances of the planets from each other correspond exactly with the intervals between these solids."

Freemasons have another symbol referring to this number in the star with five points, which is sometimes called the seal, and at others the pentangle of Solomon. It was thought that the points correspond with the five wounds of Christ. It was, however, used much earlier than the advent of our Saviour, both by Jews and heathens as an emblem of safety and health. Stukely has the following remark on this figure: " One would be apt to suspect that the Druids had a regard to the sacred symbol and mystical character of medicine, which in ancient times was thought of no inconsiderable virtue; this is a pentagonal figure formed from a triple triangle, called by the name of *Hygeia*, because it may be resolved into the Greek letters which compose that word. The Pythagoreans used it among their disciples as a mystical symbol denoting *health;* and the cabalistic Jews and Arabians had the same fancy. It is the pentalpha or pentagrammon among the Egyptians, the mark of prosperity. Antiochus Soter, going to fight against the Galatians, was advised in a dream to bear this sign upon his banner, whence he obtained a signal victory."

The attachment of the ancients to the number five was so great that they mixed five or three, but not four parts of water with their wine; and in the cure of dysentery and other complaints, Hippocrates mixed a fifth proportion of water with milk. The astrologers used five principal aspects, viz., the conjunct, the opposite, the sextile, the trigonal, and the tetragonal; from which they estimated the good or bad fortune of the native whose horoscope was before them.

The peculiarities of this number were profusely used in the science of architecture. Thus every structure was composed of five parts, viz., the foundation, the external walls, the openings of the doors and windows, the apartments, and the roof. There are five orders, and five different kinds of intercolumniations, which are determined by the proportions of height and diameter, as the pienostyle, the systyle, the eustyle, the diastyle, and the aerostyle. These are all mentioned by Vitruvius. Such a classification may have originally arisen out of an imitation of Nature, which, in many of her operations, has adopted the form of the pentad. Thus Dr Brown says, in his "Garden of Cyrus:" "Quincuncial forms and ordinations are observable in animal figurations. For to omit the hyoides or throat-bone of animals; the furcula or merry-thought in birds which supporteth the scapulæ, affording a passage for the windpipe and the gullet; the wings of flies, and disposure of their legs in their first formation from maggots, and the position of their horns, wings, and legs, in their aurelian cases; the back of the *Cimex arboreus*, found often upon trees and lesser plants, doth elegantly discover the Burgundian decussation. Besides, a large number of leaves have five divisions, and may be circumscribed by a pentagon or figure of five angles, made by right lines from the extremity of their leaves; as in the maple, vine, fig-tree. But five-leaved flowers are commonly disposed circularly about the stylus; according to the higher geometry of nature, dividing a circle by five radii, which concur not to make diameters, as in quadrilateral and sexangular intersections.

"Now the number of five is remarkable in every circle, not only as the first spherical number, but the measure of spherical motion. For spherical bodies move by fives; and every globular figure, placed upon a plane, in direct volutation returns to the first point of contaction in the first touch, accounting by the axes of the diameters or cardinal points of the four quarters thereof; and before it arrives at the same point again, it makes five circles equal unto itself, in each progress from those quarters absolving an equal circle."

The ancients considered the pentad to be a symbol of marriage and generation, because it includes the first odd, or male, and the first even, or female numbers, $3+2=5$; and was hence applied to Venus, Cytherea, Lucina, Juga, Opigura, and other deities who presided over nuptials and parturition. At weddings, the Romans had consequently a regard for this number; and as a practical display of its reference to the business in hand, five wax tapers were lighted, and placed in a conspicuous situation, as a symbol which could not be misunderstood. And the same people had a system of divination by the use of this number, which determined the good or bad fortune of the newly-married couple.

Vallancey tells us that in the "Memoirs of the Etruscan Academy of Cortona" is a drawing of a picture found in Herculaneum, representing a marriage. In the front is a sorceress casting five stones. The writer of the memoir justly thinks she is divining. The figure exactly corresponds with the first and principal cast of the Irish purim; all five are cast up, and the first catch is on the back of the hand. He has copied the drawing; on the back of the hand stands one, and the remaining four are on the ground. Opposite the sorceress is the matron, who appears to be attentive to the success of the cast. No marriage ceremony was performed without consulting the Druidess and her purim. "Auspices solebant nuptiis interesse."[1] The ancients also reckoned up five virtues of a wife, which are thus enumerated by Phintys, the daughter of Callicrates. First, in mental and bodily purity; secondly, by abstaining from excessive ornaments in dress; thirdly, by staying at home; fourthly, by refraining from the celebration of the public mysteries; and fifthly, by piety and temperance.

With a similar reference, Plato recommended that a still more significant use should be made of this number, by admitting the nuptial guests by fives.[2] This custom did not escape the penetrative satire of Rabelais. In the prophecy, by signs, of Goatnose, a deaf and dumb wizard, respecting the marriage of Panurge,[3] the following passage occurs: "Then did he lift higher up than before his said left hand, stretching out all the five fingers thereof, and severing them as wide from one another as he possibly could. Here, says Pantagruel, doth he more amply and fully insinuate unto us, by that token which he showeth forth of the quinary number, that you shall be married. Yea, that you shall not only be affi-

---

[1] Brand's Popular Antiquities, by Sir H. Ellis, vol. ii. p. 103.
[2] In Leg. iv.   [3] Book iii. c. 20.

anced, betrothed, and married, but that you shall live merrily with your wife; for Pythagoras called five the nuptial number, because it is composed of a ternary, the first of the odd, and binary, the first of the even numbers. In very deed it was the fashion of old in the city of Rome at marriage festivals to light five wax tapers; nor was it permitted to kindle any more at the magnificent nuptials of the most potent and wealthy; nor yet any fewer at the penurious weddings of the poorest and most abject in the world. Moreover, in times past, the heathen implored the assistance of five deities, helpful in five several good offices to those that were to be married. First, to Jupiter, the chief deity; to Juno, as president of the feast; to Venus, the fairest of women; to Pitho, the goddess of eloquence and persuasion; and to Diana, whose aid and succour were required in parturition."

And here the coincidence is too remarkable to be overlooked, that our blessed Saviour, in His parable of a marriage, classes the bride's attendants by fives.[1] And hence it might probably be, that the pentad was a symbol of equality and justice, not only on account of the presumed equality of the bridegroom and the bride, but also because it divides the ineffable number ten into two equal parts; and for this reason, amongst the heathen, it had the name of a demi-goddess, and was esteemed a twin.

Further, the pentad was a symbol of reconcilia-

[1] Matt. xxv. 1.

tion; the fifth element, ether, being considered free from the disturbances of the other four. It was also considered as an emblem of immortality, because it implied the fifth essence; and of sound, because the perfect fifth in music was the first diasteme. It was called providence, because it makes unequals equal; for any odd number being added to it, becomes equal; and it was identified with nature, because if multiplied by itself it returns into itself; a peculiarity which is possessed only by it and the number six. It was called justice, for justly dividing the digits, and standing in the middle between one and nine; and Nemesis, who is the messenger of justice, and the inspector of men's actions, because it harmoniously compounds the three elements, celestial, natural, and divine. Hence Plato, in his fourth book of laws, speaking on the duty of children to their parents, recommends the former to be dutiful and obedient, lest Nemesis should record their evil actions, and bring them to condign punishment.

In China, a society has recently been discovered, which boasts of great antiquity, under the name of the Triad society, and bears a great resemblance to Freemasonry. The seal, by which all the acts of the society are authenticated, is of a quinquangular figure; for five is the great mystical number of the institution. The characters on this seal are placed at the corners, and are thus explained:[1] "1. Tóo, the earth planet, or Saturn;

[1] F. Q. R., 1845, p. 165.

which, according to the Chinese, especially regards and influences the centre of the earth;—also one of the five elements. 2. Muh, the wood planet, or Jupiter, or that which reigns in the eastern part of the heavens. 3. Shwuy, the water planet, or Mercury, to which the dominion of the northern hemisphere is confided. 4. Kin, the metal planet, or Venus, who has the care of the west. 5. Ho, the fire planet, or Mars, to which the southern hemisphere is assigned. The reasons why these planets are placed at the corners of the seal may be, because they form the basis of Chinese astrological science, and because they are considered the extreme points of all created things."

In the Jewish system of religion, the gifts due to the priests were regulated by this number: (1) The heave-offering, or first-fruits; (2) the heave-offering of the Levites' tithe; (3) the cake; (4) the first of the fleece; (5) the field of possession. Again, there were five things which might not be eaten but in the camp, and afterwards only in Jerusalem; viz., (1) the breast and shoulder of the peace-offerings; (2) the heave-offering of the sacrifice of thanksgiving; (3) the heave-offering of the Nazarites' ram; (4) the firstling of the clean beast; (5) the first-fruits."[1] The Jews were forbidden to eat of their newly-planted fruit-trees till they were five years old. The princes' peace-offering was five rams, five he-goats, and five lambs; the trespass

---

[1] Pict. Bib., vol. i. p. 376, with authorities.

offering imposed on the Philistines, when they were desirous of returning the ark of alliance, was five golden emerods, and five golden mice.

There was evidently, therefore, some peculiar properties attached to the number five, even in the earliest times, as appears from the fact that Joseph gave Benjamin five changes of raiment, and his mess was five times as much as those of his brothers. And when Joseph was called on to present his brethren to Pharaoh, he did not take them all, but selected five only. And David, with a like predilection for this number, selected five pebbles from the brook as his weapons in the encounter with Goliath.

Dr Brown[1] says, that the Israelites' being forbidden to use the fruit of trees under five years old "was very agreeable unto the natural rules of husbandry; fruits being unwholesome and lask before the fourth or fifth year. They did not approve of the second day of the week, which is the feminine part of five, but in the third or masculine part; they believed that a double benediction enclosed both creations, whereof the one in some part was but an accomplishment of the other."

The articles of belief in the religion of Mahomet were five; viz., a belief in God—angels—the Prophet—the day of judgment—and predestination. It had also five positive duties; viz., prayer, fasting, purification, alms, and the pilgrimage to Mecca.

[1] Garden of Cyrus, p. 67.

When Christianity was promulgated, the same attachment to this number was transmitted by our Saviour and His apostles. Five thousand persons were fed in the wilderness with five barley loaves; and speaking of the probable effects of Christianity under some of its phases—alas! how accurately has the prophecy been accomplished!—the Saviour said, "There shall be five in one house divided—three against two, and two against three." These were the male and female numbers; and therefore He goes on to say, "The father shall be divided against the son, and the son against the father; the mother against the daughter, and the daughter against the mother; the mother-in-law against her daughter-in-law, and the daughter-in-law against her mother-in-law."[1] St Paul affirmed that he had rather speak five words in a language which was understood, than ten thousand in an unknown tongue, which is, as the commentators on the passage say, " as little as could well be spoken; *i.e.*, a simple proposition consists only of three words, and a complex one not ordinarily short of five." From these examples, the Christian Church enjoined the observance of five duties, viz., to keep holy the festivals; to observe the fasts; to attend the public services of religion; to receive the sacraments; and to adhere to the established customs and usages of the Church.

The pentad was frequently used in the composition of charms, and thus produced some very

[1] Luke xii. 52, 53.

gross superstitions. Mr Douce, in his MS. Notes, tells us of a curious custom used in Devonshire by persons afflicted with the ague. He says, "They visit at dead of night the nearest cross-road five different times, and there bury so many new-laid eggs. The visit is paid about an hour before the cold fit is expected; and they are persuaded that with the egg they shall bury the ague. If the experiment fail (and the agitation it occasions does often render it successful), they attribute it to some unlucky accident that may have befallen them in the way. In the execution of this matter they observe the strictest silence, taking care not to speak to any one whom they may happen to meet." The following curious invocation to five saints for procuring sleep is given in Bale's interlude concerning the three laws of Nature, Moses, and Christ :—

"If ye cannot slepe, but slumber,
 Geve Otes unto Saynt Uncumber,
 And Beanes in a certen number
  Unto Saynt Blase and Saynt Blythe.

"Give Onyons to Saynt Cutlake,
 And Garlycke to Saynt Cyryake,
 If ye wyll shurne Heade ake;
  Ye shall have them at Quene hyth."[1]

---

[1] Brand, *ut supra*, vol. iii. p. 149.

INFINITE DIVISIBILITY OF THE HEXAD OR DOUBLE TRIANGLE, REPRESENTING EARTH.

THE DOUBLE TRIANGLE, HEXAGON, HEXAD, OR THE NUMBER SIX.

CHAPTER VI.

THE DOUBLE TRIANGLE.

HEXAGON, HEXAD, OR THE NUMBER SIX.

"The second natural division of the circle is made by the radius, the measure of which, being transferred upon the half circumference with the compasses, always cuts it into three, or if transferred upon the whole circle, divides it absolutely into six equal portions, which is an introduction to a multitude of other no less certain divisions, and innumerable proportions between great and small figures."—La Pluche.

"The Hexagon is composed of six equilateral triangles, is equal in all its relations, and retains the quality of being infinitely divisible into similar triangles, according to the geometrical projection observed in the divisions of that trilateral figure, and may, therefore, be considered as the most perfect of all multilateral forms. From a general inquiry it will result, that the three most perfect of all geometrical diagrams are the equilateral triangle, the square, and the equal hexagon."—Hemming's Lectures.

WHAT Dr Wordsworth says about the requisites to enable an author to describe Athens, I would say, with a little alteration, of a writer on the subject of Freemasonry. "To describe Athens, a man should be an Athenian, and speak an Athenian language. He should have long looked upon its soil with a feeling of almost religious reverence. He should have regarded it as ennobled by the deeds of illustrious men, and have recognised in them his own progenitors. The records of its early history should not be to him a science; they should not have been the objects of laborious research, but should have been familiar to him from his infancy,—have sprung up, as it were, spontaneously in his mind, and have grown up with his growth. Nor should the period of its remote antiquity be to him a land of shadows—a Platonic cave in which unsubstantial forms move before his eyes as if he were entranced in a dream. To him the language of its mythology should have been the voice of truth."

The masonic writer, however, possesses some advantages over the Athenian topographer. Dr Wordsworth goes on to say: "This, we gladly confess, is not our case. We commence our description of this city with avowing the fact, that it is impossible, at this time, to convey, or entertain an idea of Athens such as it appeared of old to the eyes of one of its inhabitants. But there is another point of view from which we love to contemplate it,—one which supplies us with reflections of deeper interest, and raises in the heart sublimer emotions than could have been ever suggested in ancient days by the sight of Athens to an Athenian. *We see Athens in ruins.*" [1]

On the contrary, we rejoice because we live in times when Masonry is in a palmy and prosper-

[1] Wordsworth's Greece, p. 129.

ous state—flourishing like a green bay-tree—its principles open to the inspection of every inquirer, and its proud and lofty spirit animating every institution in existence, in every region of the globe. There it stands—a tangible reality—and therefore cannot be misrepresented by unsound theories, or false hypotheses. It occupies a situation on which the ideal cannot be permitted to set her foot; because its ground is holy, and its footstool is truth. And if Athens "issued intellectual colonies into every quarter of the world," as the learned Doctor assures us, Freemasonry has not been backward in imitating so fructifying an example; and has accomplished the very same result which he assigns to the *genius* of the Athenians—it has become immortal.

With what feelings Freemasonry in ruins might be contemplated, it would be difficult to ascertain, because it stands on too firm a basis ever to be removed. It never will be in ruins, but will last until our system shall be extinguished. If the magnificent buildings of the Acropolis had been, like Freemasonry, animated by the spirit of a true faith, they might still have existed in all their glory, and not have distributed their shattered fragments to enrich the cabinets of modern nations. Genius and intelligence may be transferred; but no people, how brave, rich, and powerful soever they may be; no monument of art, however massive, ponderous, and constructed for durability—if not supported and animated by the power of religion, and the purity of an unsophisticated worship—can escape the universal fiat of annihilation which the lips of Wisdom have pronounced against "all the works of darkness." And as Freemasonry is confessedly a system of light, there is no fear that it will ever be extinguished.

Let us, then, as good and worthy Masons, ornament our Order with deeds of virtue, truth, and brotherly love, and remember the advice of one who was inspired by wisdom, although not enlightened by revelation—

> Stat sua cuique dies ; breve et irreparabile tempus,
> Omnibus est vitæ; sed famam extendere factis,
> Hoc virtutis opus.   VIRGIL.

The hexad was considered by all nations a sacred number, because the world was created in six days ; and six of the properties of nature only are said to belong to the active dominion, to good and evil; and the planetic orb is the figure of the six properties of the spiritual world. It was represented by the double triangle, because it has six points which, amongst the Pythagoreans, denoted health, and was defined, " the consistence of a form ;" while sickness was considered the violation of it.

This figure was used by the heathen as a charm against the influence of evil demons. The Arabs believe that "communicable or contagious diseases are six: smallpox, measles, itch, putridity, melancholy, and pestilential maladies ; and that diseases engendered are also six : leprosy, hectic, epilepsy, gout, elephantiasis, and phthisis." The double triangle constituted one form of the seal of Solomon, which was so celebrated in the fictions of Arabian romance; and is used by Christians to express the two natures of Christ. With this reference, it was introduced into the cathedrals and monastic edifices of the middle ages as a conspicuous symbol; and is still to be seen in painted windows, altar screens, and other decorative parts of these sacred buildings.[1] These two intersecting triangles were also emblems of creation and redemption, fire and water, prayer and remission, repentance and forgiveness, life and death, resurrection and judgment.

The number six signified perfection of parts, because it is the only number under ten which is whole and equal in its divisions; and produces a hexagon by extending the measure of the radius of a circle six times round the circumference. The above proposition is beautifully illustrated "in the edificial palaces of bees, those monarchal spirits, who make their combs six-cornered, declining a circle, whereof many stand not close together, and completely fill the area of the place; but rather affecting a six-sided figure, whereby every cell affords a common side unto six more, and also a fit receptacle for the bee itself, which, gathering into a cylindrical figure, aptly enters its sexangular house, more nearly approaching a

---

[1] An engraving of the Dean's window in Lincoln Cathedral, in which the above symbol occurs, will be found in the Historical Landmarks of Masonry, vol. i. p. 356.

circular figure than either doth the square or triangle. And the combs themselves are so regularly contrived, that their mutual intersections make three lozenges at the bottom of every cell; which, severally regarded, make three rows of neat rhomboidal figures, connected at the angles, and so continue three several chains throughout the whole comb."[1]

Nature herself seems to affect a partiality for the hexad, in the formation of crystals; all of which are hexangular or six-cornered; for which Pliny and other ancient naturalists endeavoured in vain to assign a reason. There are three different forms, however, which crystals appear to assume: 1. The perfect columnar crystal is composed of eighteen planes, in an hexangular column, terminated by an hexangular pyramid at each end. 2. Crystals without a column are composed of two hexangular pyramids, connected at the base. 3. Imperfect crystals have usually an hexangular column, irregularly affixed to some solid body, showing also an hexangular or pentangular pyramid. "Which regular figuration," as Dr Brown observes, "hath made some to opinion, that it hath not its determination from circumscription, or as conforming unto contiguities, but rather from a seminal root and formative principle of its own, even as we observe in several other concretions."[2]

The sceptics used to amuse themselves by such arguments as these: If something be detracted

---

[1] Garden of Cyrus, p. 51.   [2] Pseudodoxia, p. 53.

The Hexad, the Symbol of Harmony. 153

from another, either an equal is detracted from an equal, a greater from a lesser, or a lesser from a greater. But none of these—therefore detraction is not possible. That detraction is not made by any of these ways is manifest. That which is detracted from another must be contained in it; but an equal is not contained in an equal, as six in six; for that which containeth ought to be greater than that which is contained. Neither is the greater contained in the lesser, as six in five; that were absurd. Neither is the lesser contained in the greater; for if five were contained in six, by the same reason, in five will be contained four; in four, three; in three, two; and in two, one. Thus six shall contain five, four, three, two, and one, which being put together make fifteen, which must be contained in six, if it be granted that the lesser is contained in the greater. In like manner, in the fifteen which is thus contained in six, will be contained thirty-five; and so by progression, infinite numbers; but it is absurd to say that infinite numbers are contained in the number six; therefore it is absurd to say that the lesser is contained in the greater.

From the harmonious movements of the planets, the hexad was considered an apt symbol of harmony; although the Pythagoreans ascribed it to a different cause. They explained it in reference to musical proportions; because 6 to 12 produced a diapason concord which contains 12 semi-tones; and 6 to 8 a diatessaron or fourth; whence the hexad was sacred to Venus, as the patroness of harmony. Macrobius, Boethius, and others, give a curious account of the accident by which Pythagoras found out these proportions; which may class with his discovery of the 47th proposition of Euclid, for which he is said to have sacrificed a hecatomb. It is thus related by Nicomachus: At one part of his life he was particularly anxious to discover some infallible instrument of music, by the use of which the entire system might be enunciated. Accidentally passing by a blacksmith's shop, he took notice of the hammers striking on the anvil; and after listening attentively for some time, he observed that the sound formed three perfect concords. Going into the shop, he made various trials himself, and found that the difference in the sounds was produced by the weight of the hammers, and not according to the force of those who struck. On this hint he tied four strings across his private room of the same substance, to each of which he hung a different weight. Then striking the strings he discovered all the concords; and that to which the greatest weight was suspended, he found to be a diapason. By the same process, he found out all the intervals.

Aristotle has used some elaborate arguments to prove that there are no figures capable of filling a place about one point, except the triangle, the square, and the hexagon; viz., by six equilateral triangles, four squares, and three hexagons. But in solids, the pyramid and cube will do the same. In this process, he shows that for equilateral triangles to fill space, it is requisite that some angles of such triangles composed about one point should make four right angles. But six equilateral triangles make four right angles; for one makes $\frac{2}{3}$ of one right angle, and therefore six make $\frac{12}{3}$ of one right, *i.e.*, four right angles. The four angles of a square, and the three angles of a hexagon make each four right angles. But no other figure can effect this, as will clearly appear, if, its angles being found, it is multiplied by any number; for the angles will always be less than, or exceed four right angles.[1]

In ancient music, a sixth was called hexachords, of which Guido divided his scale into seven; three by B quardo, two by B natural, and two by B flat. It was on this account that he disposed his gamut in three columns. In these columns were placed the three kinds of hexachords, according to their order.

A famous symbol in the Egyptian mythology, which has exercised the ingenuity of many commentators, was the globe, serpent, and wings, of which there were six various ways of disposing the several parts: (1.) From the lower part of an annulus surmounted by two wings rising perpendicularly, two serpents issue in opposite directions. The whole is enclosed within a circle. (2.) The winged globe alone without the serpent. The wings expanded. This figure might be intended to represent the rays of the rising sun, which are, poetically, his wings. From this

[1] Taylor's Proclus, p. 17.

sacred figure, which represented the deity of the Gentiles, was probably borrowed the sublime metaphor of Malachi—The SUN OF RIGHTEOUSNESS shall arise with healing in His WINGS. (3.) A simple globe without wings, from which issue two serpents. (4.) A winged globe, through the lower part of which passes a serpent. (5.) A plain globe, over which passes the serpent. (6.) The same as the first without the circumscribing circle.[1]

In the Theosophic or Rosicrucian systems of Freemasonry, the number six was referred to the rainbow, because it displays that number of prismatic colours; and from this principle they deduced the following argument, which was used in their lectures: "The rainbow is a token of God's Covenant, a representation to man of all the three principles out of which he was created —viz., the red and dark brown betoken the first principle, *i.e.*, the dark, fire world, the kingdom of God's anger. The white and yellow show the second principle, the majestic colour, the holy world, God's love. The green and blue is the third principle's colour—the blue from chaos, the green from saltpetre, where, in the flagrat, the sulphur and mercury do sever, and produce various colours, which betoken the inward worlds hidden in the four elements. The rainbow is a further symbol of Christ appearing in the three principles, as the Judge of mankind. In the first, or fiery, all evil things shall be swallowed up. In

[1] Dean, Serpent., p. 53.

the second, or that of light, He will defend the good, in love and meekness, from the flames of fire. In the third, or kingdom of nature, the humanity of the Judge is typified, and shows His impartiality in passing sentence on every man according to his works."

In one of the degrees of ineffable Masonry, the same number is denoted by the double equilateral triangle, which is there said to refer to the six peculiar branches of the noblest office in the Temple—viz., (1) To survey the constitutional rolls previous to their being deposited in the archives of Masonry, or hollow pillars of the temple; (2) to see that the stones fitted into each other with perfect exactness and geometrical truth; (3) to inspect the Holy Place, and (4) the Sanctum Sanctorum; (5) the ark of the covenant; and (6) all the other utensils thus emblematically pointed to by the double equilateral triangle.

Like the pentad, the number six was an ancient symbol of marriage, being formed by the multiplication of 3, the male, with 2, the female number; and from this cause it was named Conciliation, because it links or conciliates, by such involution, male and female into one body, husband and wife. And the Pythagoreans extended the influence of this number to the periods of gestation. They contended that "generally there are two kinds of births; one lesser, of seven months, which comes into the world 207 days after conception; the other greater, of ten months, which is brought forth in the 274th day. The first and lesser is chiefly contained in the number six; for the two first periods of 6 and 8 days make the first concord, diatessaron; the third period is of 9 days, in which time it is made flesh; these to the first 6 are in sesquialtera proportion, and make the second concord, diapente. Then follow 12 days more, in which the body is fully formed; these to the same 6 consist in duple proportion, and make the diatessaron concord. These four numbers, 6, 8, 9, 12, added together, make 35 days. It is not without reason, therefore, that the number six is the foundation of generation, for the Greeks call it *Teleion*, or perfect, because its three parts, $\frac{1}{6}$, $\frac{1}{3}$, and $\frac{1}{2}$ (*i.e.*, 1, 2, 3), make it perfect. The above 35 being multiplied by 6 make 210 days, in which the maturity is fulfilled."[1]

The cabalistic theologians say that this number affects the operation of the senses during sleep; because they consider sleep to be the sixtieth part of death. "The soul," they say, "being pure and holy, ascends in contemplation by degrees to the communication with angels, by which future events are often revealed to it; whence descending, after being perfectly purified, it brings down, unmixed, the knowledge that has been manifested to it — these are prophetic dreams; for, from imagination not entering into them, they deviate in nothing from the truth. If the soul be not perfectly pure, it meets with

[1] Stanley, Pyth., p. 103.

nothing but mixed and vain phantoms; and if impure, it does not ascend at all, but remains confused by demons and unclean spirits."

The number 666, or the hexad thrice repeated, has engaged the attention of cabalistical theologians for 1800 years, as the mysterious Apocalyptic number; and many and various have been its interpretations. "It has greatly perplexed the curious," says Calmet, " to know whether the name of the beast should be written in Hebrew, Syriac, Greek, or Latin; whether his name be that of his person, or of his dignity, or that which his followers should give him; or that which he will deserve by his crimes. There are many conjectures in this matter; and almost all commentators have tried their skill, without being able to say, positively, that any one has succeeded in ascertaining the true mark of the beast, or the number of his name." Calmet has enumerated fourteen different interpretations, and concludes by saying, "Since the number 666 is found in names the most sacred, the wisest and safest way is to be silent." I subjoin five instances of the application of this number, to show how uncertain it may be—viz., Dioclesian, Julian the Apostate, Luther, Abinu Kadescha Papa, our holy father the Pope, and Elion Adonai Jehovah Kadosh, the Most High, the Lord, the Holy God. And a recent masonic writer (*F. M. Mag.*, 1857, p .706) says, that by means of a rational interpretation of this number, the mysteries of the triangle and square are united in one masonic symbol, typical of the chief essential attributes of the Great Geometrician of the Universe.

"There was an ancient and almost immemorial tradition among the Jews that the world was to last only 6000 years. They divided the ages, during which it was to continue, in the following manner: Two thousand years were to elapse before the law took place; two thousand were to be passed under the law; and two thousand under the Messiah. Indeed, this sexmillennial duration of the world was, it is probable, too much the belief of the ancient fathers, who conceived that, as the creation was formed in six days, reckoning according to that assertion in the Psalms, that every day is with God as a thousand years, and was concluded by a grand Sabbath, or day of Almighty rest; so the world was ordained to last only during the revolution of six thousand years."[1] Some visionaries, however, have been bold enough to name the precise periods when these six chiliads commence and terminate, and have made each of them correspond with some great historical epoch: 1. From the creation to the flood. 2. To the promise made to Abraham. 3. To the commencement of David's kingdom. 4. To the Babylonish captivity. 5. To the advent of Christ. 6. To the day of judgment.

But a reference to facts will prove this calculation erroneous. It is true the hypothesis that the duration of the world will continue six ages

[1] Maur. Ind. Ant., vol. v. p. 831.

may be quite consistent with analogy and the revealed will of God, but the length of the intermediate periods vary considerably ; for the first period, from the creation to the deluge, contains 1656 years; the second, from the flood to Abraham, if it be considered to terminate at the commencement of his peregrination, has only 427 years; the third, to the beginning of David's kingdom at the death of Saul, has 866 years; the fourth, to the Babylonish captivity, 448 years ; the fifth, to the advent of Christ, 602 years ; and the sixth is now incomplete.

On this subject, I remember reading a pamphlet many years ago, which interested me by its ingenuity ; and as the events which it commemorates' are most of them comprised in the historical lectures of Masonry, I will give a brief outline of it, so far as my recollection will bear me out. The author commenced by instituting a comparison between the days of the week and the millenaries of the world, in illustration of the text, " One day is with the Lord as a thousand years, and a thousand years as one day."[1] The first day of the week, Sunday, or the first thousand years, was, according to this author, opened by the creation of the world, and closed with the translation of Enoch; an event, one would think, which could scarcely fail to strike a wicked race with wonder, awe, and reverence, and produce the effect of turning them from their wicked-

[1] 2 Pet. iii. 8.

ness to worship the living God. It failed to do so; and the prevalence of fraud and violence brought on its destruction by an universal deluge.

The next chiliad, or Monday, the second day of the week, he terminates with the mission of Abraham; and opens the third millennium, or Tuesday, with a series of gracious revelations which heralded the establishment of the Jewish Church, a type of a more perfect dispensation which would ultimately be revealed from on high. During this period, the Mosaic dispensation was promulgated, and the law firmly established for the civil and religious government of the Hebrew nation, who were delivered from their cruel bondage in Egypt, and received possession of the Promised Land as an inheritance.

The next millennial period, corresponding with Wednesday, commenced with the construction of Solomon's Temple, and the attainment of that exalted summit of prosperity and power which, as had been promised to Abraham, his posterity should attain. This period commenced gloriously for the Jews; but its progress was marked with calamity. Their kingdom was taken from them, and they were deprived of the power of governing their own people. At the period when their sufferings were the most severe, and the sceptre had for ever departed from Judah, a still more refulgent era dawned upon the world. The day-spring from on high called the bright Morning

Star—Orieus—the Sun of Righteousness—the Messiah so long promised to the Jews—enlightened the benighted atmosphere at the commencement of the fifth millennium, or Thursday. Now the fulness of time was come; the prophecies of the Messiah or Shiloh were fulfilled; the everlasting gospel was preached; and the work of redemption completed by Him of whom Moses and the prophets did write—Jesus of Nazareth, the King of the Jews.

The sixth chiliad, corresponding with Friday, opened in darkness. Literature and religion were both at a low ebb. Emperors and potentates were ignorant of letters, and the nobility of every Christian country were few of them able to read or write their own names. Charlemagne and Barbarossa, famous for conquest, were neither of them capable of writing their own despatches, or reading them when written; and some of the popes were equally illiterate. Under such circumstances, religion would necessarily be exchanged for superstition. The controlling spirits were barbarous and ferocious; for they had no mitigating principles to fall back upon. The yoke of superstition was always burdensome; and by its corrective policy—such as it was—the iron chiefs of every Christian nation were overawed, and subjected to the influence of an hierarchy more ambitious and insatiable than themselves.

Such was the opening of the sixth millennial period, in the year 1000 of the Christian era;

about which time vast improvements in ecclesiastical architecture were on the eve of being accomplished; and the Freemasons spread over the face of every country where the religion of Jesus was professed, the proudest specimens of human taste and genius which have distinguished any age or nation since the world was made. From the commencement of the period in which we live, science and learning have rapidly increased, and the day of perfect civilisation has arrived. We are drawing near to the close of this period, and the opening of a glorious millennium—prefigured by the Jewish Sabbath—the day on which God rested from His labours at the creation of the world. This period will also continue a thousand years, when Christ will reign in glory over the whole society of the redeemed, and Satan be cast, bound, into the bottomless pit.

Many of the primitive Christians, and particularly Barnabas, the companion of St Paul, maintain this opinion. The latter writer, in his Catholic Epistle, says: "God made in six days the works of His hands, and He finished them on the seventh day; and He rested on the seventh day, and sanctified it. Consider then, my children, what that signifies—He finished them in six days. The meaning of it is this—that in 6000 years the Lord God will bring all things to an end; for with Him one day is a thousand years, as Himself testifieth. Therefore in six days shall all things be accomplished. And what is this that He saith—and He rested on the seventh day? He meaneth this—that when His Son shall come, and abolish the season of the wicked one, and judge the ungodly, and change the sun and the moon and the stars, then He shall gloriously rest on that seventh day."

REMARKABLE PROPERTIES OF THE HEPTAD, SEPTENARY, OR HEPTAGON.

THE HEPTAGON, SEPTENARY, OR THE NUMBER SEVEN.

CHAPTER VII.

THE HEPTAGON.

SEPTENARY, OR THE NUMBER SEVEN.

"THE number seven was held to be sacred by the Hebrews, and also by the Mussulmans to this day, who reckon seven climates, seven seas, seven heavens, and as many hells. According to Rabbis and Mussulman authors, the body of Adam was made of seven handfuls of mould, taken from the seven stages of the earth."—WILFORD.

"How old are you?—Under seven."—OLD LECTURES OF MASONRY.

"There are seven mysterious voyages necessary for the reception of the Master Mason's degree—1. The candidate is instructed in Music, Poetry, and Painting. 2. He is made acquainted with the sciences of Geology, Geography, and Natural History. 3. He is taught Theology, Medicine, and Jurisprudence. The four other voyages instruct him in the still higher sciences."—ROSENBERG.

WHILE engaged on the subject of numbers, we cannot fail to be struck with its illustration during the prevalence in this country of the rage for lottery speculations, when everything was supposed to depend on the choice of a fortunate figure. There are some apposite remarks on this fever of the mind in the *Spec-*

tator, No. 191, which show its workings. The writer says: " Caprice very often acts in the place of reason, and forms to itself some groundless, imaginary motive, where real and substantial ones are wanting. I know a well-meaning man who risked his good fortune upon the number of the year of our Lord, whatever it might be. I am acquainted with a tacker that would give a good deal for the number 134. On the contrary, I have been told of a certain zealous Dissenter who, being a great enemy to Popery, and believing that bad men are the most fortunate in this world, will lay two to one on the number 666 against any other number; because, says he, it is the number of the beast. Several would prefer the number 12,000 before any other, as it is the number of pounds in the great prize; and a premium was publicly advertised for the ticket numbered 132. In short, some are pleased to find their own age in the number; some that they have got a number that makes a pretty appearance in the ciphers; and others because it is the same number that succeeded in the last lottery; while some are governed in the choice of a number by dreams. Each of these, upon no other grounds, thinks he stands the fairest for the great lot, and that he is possessed of what may not be improperly called the Golden Number."

The Pythagoreans considered seven to be a religious number and perfect, and consequently entitled to veneration; although, strictly speaking, no number can be perfect, unless it is capable of being formed from the sum of its aliquot parts. In the Continental system of Freemasonry, it is termed a "nombre mystique et respectable." We find in our own Scriptures such an abundant use of it, as to convince the most inveterate sceptic that it occupied no unimportant station in the ordinances of divine worship, both amongst the patriarchs and Jews; and it appears to have been held in equal estimation by the early Christian writers.[1]

In the spurious Freemasonry of the Greeks and Romans, it represented good fortune; and referred to the periodical changes of the moon, which alters its appearance every seven days. And with this interpretation, and governed by lunary influence, the critical and climacterical points in the life and fortunes of man were probably determined. Opinions appear to differ in the details, although they agree in the principle. Thus, some think that seven times seven is the most dangerous period of life; others contend for seven times nine, and some for nine times nine; while others conceive seven times nine to be the least dangerous. Varro divided the days of man into five portions; Hippocrates into seven; and Solon into ten; yet probably their divisions were to be received with latitude, and their considerations not strictly to be confined unto their last unities.

[1] See the Hist. Landm. Mas., Lect. xx. vol. i. p. 512.

When Hippocrates divided our life into seven degrees or stages, he made the end of the first period seven years; of the second, fourteen; of the third, twenty-eight; of the fourth, thirty-five; of the fifth, forty-seven; of the sixth, fifty-six; and of the seventh, the last year, whenever it happeneth. Herein we may observe, he maketh not his divisions precisely by seven and nine, and omits the great climacterical. Besides, there is between every one at least the latitude of seven years, in which space or interval, *i.e.*, either in the third or fourth, whatever falleth out is equally verified in the whole degree, as though it had happened in the seventh.[1] And hence this number was called *Telesphoros*, because by it all mankind are led to their end.[2] This superstition was not confined to those ages and nations, but has descended in all its force to our own times.

The number seven was also a symbol of custody, because it was figured or believed (no matter which) that the government of the world was in the custody of the seven planets. And from this fiction Pythagoras formed his doctrine of the spheres. He called that a tone which is the distance of the moon from the earth; from the moon to Mercury half a tone; from thence to Venus the same; from Venus to the sun, a tone and a half; from the sun to Mars a tone; from thence to Jupiter half a tone; from Jupiter to

---

[1] Brown, Pseudodoxia, p. 249.   [2] Philo de mund. opif.

Saturn half a tone; and thence to the zodiac a tone;—thus making seven tones, which he called a diapason harmony. Now it is well known that there are in music seven original notes; "but these are capable of being transposed into situations more acute or grave, still retaining their number and order; and though the octave contain twelve semitonic intervals, and every interval may be infinitely divided, still the eighth note of every division, diatonically reckoning, will produce a similar sound. From these seven sounds, taken in various successions, and different degrees of time or measure, all melody is formed; and the sounds being fixed in themselves, nothing is left to the choice of the composer, but the order and time in which they shall succeed each other."[1]

Addison had some reference to the above system when he wrote his celebrated paraphrase on the nineteenth Psalm; which contains a representation of the sun, moon, and stars continually employed in announcing the wonderful works of the Creator:—

> For ever singing, as they shine,
> The hand that made us is divine.

The heptad was considered to be the number of a virgin, because it is unborn; without a father (the first odd number 3) or a mother (the first even number 2), but proceeding directly from the

[1] Busby, Dict. Mus., Introd., xii.

monad, which is the origin and crown of all things. On this principle the Arabs, and most Eastern nations, usually name and circumcise their children on the seventh day after their birth; and at the age of seven years teach them to read and pray. The number seven being thus introduced into the common offices of Arab life, it is probable that the seven degrees of initiation used by the Eastern order of Assassins, established by the Sheik Hassan ben Sabah, originated. These were—1. The profane. 2. The aspirants. 3. The devoted. 4. The companions. 5. The dais or ministers. 6. The rulers. 7. The grand priors.

The same number was sacred to several male and female deities, as, for instance, to Minerva, because she was fatherless and motherless, being hewn out of the skull of Jupiter with an axe. It was consecrated to Mars, because he had seven attendants, Bellona, Anger, Clamour, Fear, Terror, Discord, and Fury. It was a symbol of Osiris, because his body was said to have been divided into seven parts, according to some accounts, and twice seven according to others, by Typhon. It was also sacred to Apollo or the sun, because being placed in the midst of the seven planets, they proceed harmoniously together through the vast expanse, whence the poets have feigned that the instrument on which Apollo plays is a harp with seven strings. Being thus made an emblem of the chief deity, the Greek poet says:—

> Επτα με, &c.
> Seven sounding letters sing the praise of me,
> The immortal God, the Almighty Deity;
> Father of all that cannot weary be.
> I am the eternal viol of all things,
> Whereby the melody so sweetly rings
> Of heavenly music.

Lightfoot, after quoting the above lines, adds, "What these seven letters are that do express God is easy to guess, that they be the letters of the name of JEHOVAH."

The use of the number seven has not been confined to any age or nation, as may be gathered from the seven vases in the Temple of the Sun near the ruins of Babian, in Upper Egypt; the seven altars which burned continually before the god Mithras in many of his temples; the seven holy fanes of the Arabians; the seven bobuns of perfection exhibited in the religious code of the Hindoos; with the defective geographical knowledge of the same people, which circumscribed the whole earth within the compass of seven peninsulas surrounded by seven seas; the seven planets; the Jewish Sephiroth of seven splendours; the seven Gothic deities; the seven worlds of the Indians and Chaldeans; the seven virtues, cardinal and theological; the seven constellations mentioned by Hesiod and Homer; the seven wise men; the seven wonders of the world; the seven cities which contended for the birth of Homer; the seven prismatic colours; the seven notes in music, and a host of other references to the same number, which it will be unnecessary to adduce here, because they may be found in the twentieth Lecture of the "Historical Landmarks of Masonry."

This universal veneration for the heptad might probably derive its origin, even among the heathen nations who were unacquainted with the Mosaic writings, from the creation of the world; for the seventh day was looked upon as sacred throughout the whole world.[1] Hesiod uses the words, "The seventh is a sacred day;" and Linus says, "On the seventh day all things were finished; the seventh is beautiful; it is the origin of all things; it is perfect and complete." Theophilus, Bishop of Antioch, writing to Autolycus, has this remarkable passage: "The greatest part of the heathens are ignorant of the *name* of the seventh day, nevertheless all men celebrate it." Josephus against Apion affirms, that "there is no Grecian city, nor barbarian, nor any nation where the custom of observing the seventh day has not reached."

The Jewish cabalists, as I have already observed, believed in the existence of seven Sephiroth, which they denominated Strength, Mercy, Beauty, Victory, Glory, Foundation, and Kingdom. The benefit of these divine splendours were communicated by gradations, and

---

[1] See Clem. Alex. Strom., viii.—Euseb. in the Fragments of Aristobulus; as well as the passages out of Hesiod, Callimachus, and others to the same purpose.

compared to ascending the steps of a ladder, on the summit of which were the three hypostases of the divine nature, surmounted by a crown of glory and the throne of God. These were considered equivalent to seven heavens or divisions of the celestial abodes. They had also seven hells, because they say that Gehenna, the place of abode for wicked spirits and sinful men, is mentioned in Scripture under so many different appellations. They were called, Infernus, Perditio, Profundum, Taciturnitas, Umbra mortis, Terra inferior, and Terra sitiens.

In like manner, the followers of Mahomet had their seven heavens and seven hells. Of the former, the first is described as formed of emerald, the second of white silver, the third of large white pearls, the fourth of ruby, the fifth of red gold, the sixth of yellow jacinth, and the seventh of shining light. Some assert Paradise to be in the seventh heaven; others contend that next above the seventh heaven are seven seas of light; then an undefinable number of veils or separations of different substances, seven of each kind; and then Paradise, which consists of seven stages one above another—the first called the mansion of glory, the second the mansion of peace, the third the garden of rest, the fourth the garden of eternity, the fifth the garden of delight, the sixth the garden of Paradise, and the seventh the garden of perpetual abode, or of Eden—this overlooking all the former, and canopied by the throne of God.

In like manner, the seven hells are situated one beneath the other. The first of these, according to the general opinion, is destined for the reception of wicked Mahometans, the second for Christians, the third for Jews, the fourth for Sabians, the fifth for the Magians, the sixth for the idolaters, and the seventh for hypocrites. To complete the system, the Mahometans believed in the existence of seven earths, each forming a story or gradation above the other; the earth which we inhabit being the next in succession beneath the lowest heaven, and the first hell is beneath the lowest earth. And hence the Arabians assigned to the earth seven climates, and to heaven seven spheres. "Each of these earths is inhabited: the first by men, genii, brutes, &c.; the second by a suffocating wind; the third by the stones of Jahennum or hell; the fourth by the sulphur of the infernal regions; the fifth by serpents; the sixth by scorpions, in colour and size like black mules, and with tails like spears; and the seventh by Iblees and his troops."[1]

According to this system of belief, the universe was divided into three great portions, and subdivided into twenty-one steps or degrees, situated at equal distances from each other; the lower seven being places of punishment; the interme-

[1] Lane, Arabian Nights, vol. i. pp. 20-24.

diate seven, places of probation; and the upper seven, places of reward. Pythagoras and Plato had some such system in their notion of seven zones, which extended from the earth to the supreme heavens,[1] and it is glanced at in the writings of St Paul.[2]

The Theosophic philosophy, which was copiously introduced into the counterfeit Masonry practised on the Continent during the last century, counted seven properties in man—viz., 1. The divine golden man. 2. The inward holy body from fire and light, like pure silver. 3. The elemental man. 4. The mercurial growing paradisiacal man. 5. The martial soul-like man. 6. The venerine, according to the outward desire. 7. The solar man, an inspector of the wonders of God. They had also seven fountain spirits, or powers of nature, called Binding, Attraction, Anguish, Fire, Light, Sound, and Body. According to which the seven royal stars are like vowels or spirits of letters; and the innumerable others are like consonants, forming an infinite variety of syllables and words; for as words are the opening of the secret locked up in the mind, so are the stars the opening of the dark mystery or chaos shut up in the anguish chambers. And as the various properties of the several principles are couched in and expressed by the vowels and spirits of the letters peculiar to them, so the seven

---

[1] Pliny, l. ix. c. 21.
[2] 2 Cor. xii. 2.

royal stars are suited in and qualified by the three principles and seven properties of the eternal nature.

The same philosophy, which formed the general material from which Cagliostrô, Mesmer, Peuvret, and other charlatans of the last century, constructed their several systems of Freemasonry, professed also to believe that the gifts and graces of the Holy Spirit were seven in number—viz., wisdom, understanding, counsel, grace, knowledge, piety, and the fear of God; and that there were the same number of works of mercy to which a reward would be attached, *i.e.*, to instruct the ignorant; to correct offenders; to confirm the wavering; to comfort the afflicted; to suffer patiently; to forgive injuries; and to pray for enemies. In the same system, there were accounted seven virtues—humility, liberality, chastity, quietness, temperance, patience, and devotion; and seven deadly sins—pride, covetousness, luxury, envy, gluttony, anger, and sloth.

In the French system of symbolical Masonry, as it is now practised, the number seven in the Fellow Craft's degree is explained by a reference not only to the seven days of the creation, and the seven years employed in building the Temple of Solomon, but also to the seven virtues which every good Mason ought to practise without intermission. These differ slightly from the former, and consist of wisdom, strength, beauty, power, humility, glory, and honour; and seven vices which he ought to tread under his feet—hatred, discord, pride, indiscretion, perfidy, rashness, and calumny. The seven virtues recommended by the same order are, friendship, unity, submission, discretion, fidelity, prudence, and temperance. They referred the same number also, as we do, to the seven liberal sciences. With respect to the latter, a curious tale is told by M. d'Autun on learned incredulity, where it is said that the use of the Arabian numerals were imported from Spain by Pope Silvester, to be used in magical ceremonies; for it should appear that magic was publicly taught in the recesses of a deep cavern at Salamanca. This Domdaniel is said to have been founded by Hercules, and that seven arts of enchantment were taught therein. Sir Walter Scott, in his " Lay of the Last Minstrel," observes, that " if the classic reader inquires where Hercules learned magic, he may consult *Les faicts et proesses du noble et vaillant Hercules,* where he will learn that the fable of his aiding Atlas to support the heavens arose from the said Atlas having taught Hercules, the noble knight-errant, the seven liberal sciences, and, in particular, that of judicial astrology." [1]

I shall here close my brief remarks upon this number, because it is copiously explained in the

[1] Lay, canto ii. note 12.

"Historical Landmarks of Freemasonry."[1] There is no other number which is so freely used by the professors of every religion, both true and false. It was uniformly considered to be worthy of veneration, and there appears to have been ample cause for it, in the profuse use of it which is contained in the directions of the Almighty respecting the customs and ceremonies of the Jewish Church. This people, however, had many other superstitions besides a predilection for the number seven as the harbingers of good-luck. The following is to our purpose, because it embodies a masonic custom: "Some of the modern Jews are particularly careful, while dressing themselves in a morning, to put on the right stocking and right shoe first, without tying them; then to put on the left, and so return to the right; that so they may begin and end with the right side, which they account to be the most fortunate."[2]

It may be observed here, in reference to the above practice, that naked feet were a sign of mourning, and also a mark of respect. Moses had naked feet at the burning bush; and it is believed that the priests served both in the tabernacle and temple in the same manner. It is said further that the Israelites were not permitted to enter the holy place except they were divested of their shoes. It was customary to loose the latchet

[1] Lect. xx.
[2] Leo. Modena, p. 17.

of the shoes when in the house, and fasten them when going from home. Thus St Peter[1] was commanded to gird himself, and bind on his sandals, when he was miraculously delivered from prison. With some nations, it was a custom when they entered a temple to set the right foot upon the first step. And the practice of taking off the shoes was ultimately converted to the purposes of superstition. It was believed by the Romans that if seven women walked barefoot round a garden, it would be free from caterpillars and other destructive insects. Sorceresses used to cast off their shoes during their incantations. The aborigines of Peru were of opinion that it was sinful to enter the Temple of the Sun without first taking off their shoes; which they considered to be the greatest proof they could possibly give of their unfeigned humility.

This remarkable practice, so extensive in its operation, was most probably derived from the Jewish law, in which it is directed, that if a husband dies without issue, then his brother shall be at liberty to marry his widow, or give her permission to marry any other person. The latter is called Caliga, and the sign is, "loosing the shoe." A similar custom was used by the same people in the conveyance of a title to an estate. The person who sold or conveyed it pulled off one of his shoes, and in open court delivered it to the purchaser, thereby signifying that he had full

[1] Acts xii. 8.

right to walk, enter into, and tread upon the land as his own proper and entire possession. Sometimes the right-hand glove, and sometimes a handkerchief, is substituted for the shoe.

Michaelis,[1] speaking on this subject, says, that "in the age of David this usage had become antiquated; for the writer introduces it as an unknown custom of former times, in the days of David's great-grandfather. I have not been able to find any farther trace of it in the East, nor yet has the Danish travelling mission to Arabia, as Captain Niebuhr himself informs me. Bynæus, in his 'Book de Calceis Hebræorum,' treats of it at great length; but, excepting the mere conjectures of modern literature, he gives no account of the origin of this strange symbol of the transfer of property. In the time of Moses, it was so familiar, that *barefooted* was a term of reproach, and probably signified a man that had sold everything, a spendthrift, and a bankrupt; and in Deuteronomy we find that Moses allowed it to be applied to the person who would not marry his brother's widow. Could it have been an Egyptian custom, as we do not find it again in the East? The Egyptians, when they adored the Deity, had no shoes on; and of this the Pythagoreans gave the following explanation. The man who came naked from his mother's womb should appear naked before his Creator; for God hears those alone who are not

[1] Vol. i. p. 434.

burdened with anything extrinsic. Among the Egyptians, too, barefooted was equivalent to naked, and naked synonymous with having no property but one's self."

MYSTERIOUS REFERENCES OF THE OGDOAD OR CUBE, REPRESENTING AIR.

THE CUBE, OGDOAD, OCTAEDRON, OR THE NUMBER EIGHT.

CHAPTER VIII.

THE CUBE.

OGDOAD, OCTAEDRON, OR THE NUMBER EIGHT.

> "When in his ark of gopher-wood
> Noah rode buoyant on the flood,
> O'erwhelmed with sad despair and woe,
> A guilty race sunk down below.
> With blest Omnipotence its guide,
> The mastless ark did safely ride,
> And on the mount, from danger free,
> Did rest the whole fraternity."
> *From an unpublished* MASONIC ODE.

"THE double cubical figure hath always been a lively representation of the chief attributes of the Divinity, as well as that which constitutes the most capital problem in Masonry; which is that of doubling the cube, and was first proposed by the oracle at Delphus to those who asked him what was necessary to be done to stop the pestilence which then raged amongst them. He told them to double his altar, and the plague should cease."—OLD R. A. LECTURES.

WHEN the theory was once established that names and numbers bore a mutual relation to each other, it became a favourite employment with the cabalists — Jewish, Christian, and Mahometan—to trace by numbers the mysterious reference of certain remarkable names. Thus the Egyptian Mercury *Thouth*, the representative of wisdom, or moral strength, was denoted by the number 1218, the era A.A.C., in which Samson flourished, who was the greatest example of physical strength the world ever produced; θ being 9; ω, 800; υ, 400; θ, 9. The monogram of Christ crucified, or I.H.T., or more properly I.H̄. The former signifying the two first letters of the Greek name of Christ, and the latter His cross, was found in the number 318; *i.e.*, I, 10; H, 8; and T, 300; being the date of the abolition of that kind of death which was inflicted on the Saviour of mankind. Again, the Hebrew letters of the name *Jabo-Shiloh*, or "Shiloh shall come," are numerically the same as those of the word Messiah; whence it was concluded that Shiloh and Messiah were one and the same person. By a similar process the Creator ('Η'Αρχη) was denoted by the number 737; and Lateinos, according to Irenæus, was found in the number, 6 6 6. "*Sed et Lateinos nomen habet sexcentorum sexaginta sex numerum; et valde verisimile est, quoniam novissimum regnum hoc habet vocabulum. Latini enim sunt qui nunc regnant; sed non in hoc nos gloriabimur.*"[1]

The Arabs, according to Lane, have a method of divination, used at marriages, to determine whether the parties will be happy. This is done by "adding together the numerical values of the

---

[1] Iren., l. v. c. 30.

letters composing his or her name, and that of the mother, and subtracting from twelve the whole sum, if it be less than twelve, or if larger, dividing it by twelve. Thus is obtained the number of the sign. The twelve signs, commencing with Aries, correspond respectively with the elements of fire, earth, air, and water, three times repeated. If the signs of the two parties indicate the same element, it is inferred that they will agree; but if they indicate different elements, the inference is that the one will be affected by the other, in the same manner as these elements are; thus if the element of the man is fire, and that of the woman water, he will be subject to her rule. Another method is to subtract the numerical values of the two names one from the other; and if the remainder is an uneven number, the inference is unfavourable; but if even, the reverse."

The ogdoad, according to the philosophers, is the first cube, consisting of six sides and eight angles; and, as was asserted by the Pythagoreans, is the only number under ten which can be pronounced evenly even. This, however, is not strictly correct; for evenly even means divisible by any other even number without a remainder, which will equally apply to the number four. It does not appear to have been very highly esteemed by the followers of Pythagoras, although the deluge was commemorated in their mysterious observances, and eight persons were believed to have been saved in the ark from destruction during that terrible event. Amongst the Jews, it appears to have been the number of circumcision, because that ceremony took place on the eighth day; and with the cabalists it was the number of Jesod or Mercury, the dry water, or water of immersion, in which lay the whole foundation of the art of transmuting metals. They observe eight orders of purification of the baser metal, because the number of the word Zachu, or purity, is equal to 33, which being multiplied by 8, the number of Jesod, produces 264, the number of the word Jordan.[1]

The Pythagorean philosophers taught that the cube proceeded from the tetractys. But they conceived that some third principle was necessary to unite the other two; for *matter* and *form* do not flow one into another spontaneously, because the matter of one substance does not receive the form of the other without something to impress it. As, for instance, when the soul departs out of a man, the body does not become brass or iron; neither is wool made out of a stone. There must be some third principle to unite them; and that principle can be nothing else but the Deity.

The number eight had other references which it may be useful to point out. It signified the harmony produced by love and friendship, because the perfect diapason constitutes the unison of two notes in the same sound, which is termed an octochord, and comprises eight notes and seven degrees. This was a symbol of the intimate union which

[1] F. Q. R., 1838, p. 448.

subsists between two minds which are knit and joined together by these two genial affections. Pythagoras had a musical instrument which he denominated an octochord, comprehending the two disjunct tetrachords expressed by the letters E, F, G, A, B, C, D, E. This number was invested with the name of several heathen deities, both male and female; as Neptune, Cybele, Rhea, &c.

The Pythagoreans held that there are in man eight organs of knowledge; viz., sense, phantasy, art, opinion, prudence, science, wisdom, and mind; which constituted an inexhaustible source of disquisition in the Pythagorean Lodges. In like manner, the Christian system presents us with eight beatitudes: poverty of spirit; mourning; meekness; desire of righteousness; mercy; purity of heart; the peacemaker; and suffering for the sake of righteousness.[1]

This number was highly esteemed in Egypt; and in the sacred processions, a vessel or boat was carried containing eight persons, in reference to the Noetic ogdoad; and Herodotus informs us that the Egyptians had eight great gods. Now, although this may not be strictly correct, yet it shows that eight was esteemed a sacred number; for the tradition was universal, that the world had been destroyed by a deluge of waters, and eight persons preserved in a vessel which floated on its surface.

The legend of initiation, or the account of the

[1] Matt. v. 1-10.

death of Osiris by the contrivance of Typhon, has been variously interpreted. In one sense it is sideral, and in another diluvian; and their union may approximate nearest to the truth. It is, however, certain, that a knowledge of the universal deluge was preserved in the spurious Freemasonry of ancient times; and the tradition is not obscurely intimated or conveyed by symbols of doubtful interpretation, but plainly declared and explicitly proclaimed. The days of mourning for the aphanism were usually $5 \times 8 = 40$; and the rites of probation were forty days, in allusion to the time which marked the increase of the diluvian waters. This was accompanied amongst the Eastern nations by a curious ceremony. They held that sin being the pollution of man's soul, regeneration could only be produced by bathing in pure water, under the influence of a particular planet. These ablutions were to be accompanied by many trifling, and even ridiculous, observances, the absence of any one of which would render the whole ceremony inefficacious. According to Mr Colebrooke, "the aspirant was taught to repeat mentally the names of the seven worlds; and after sipping a little of the water, he was to cast some of it eight times into the air, repeating the prayer of ablution. If he chanced to spit or sneeze during the performance of this ceremony, he was obliged immediately to apply the forefinger of his right hand to his ear; in compliance with the maxim,—after sneezing, spitting, blowing the nose, sleeping, putting on apparel, or other unclean act, you must not perform your ablutions till you have touched your right ear."

From this event, three supplemental degrees of Masonry have been constructed, called respectively the Royal Ark Mariners, the Noachites, and the Ark and the Dove. The former enters philosophically in its ordinary lectures on the subject of the salvation of Noah and his seven companions in the ark, if they have undergone no alteration of late years. The lectures of this degree, however, vary so considerably in different Lodges that nothing certain can be pronounced respecting them; except that they relate to Noah and his family—the construction of the ark—and the planting of nations.

The degree of the Noachites includes circumstances which extended from the deluge to the dispersion of mankind; the principal of which are, the building of the tower of Babel, the confusion of tongues, and the planting of nations; together with the death, and presumed sepulture, of the chief architect in a cavern or vault on the continent of Europe. Respecting this degree, the following account is given in Dr Mackey's "Freemason's Lexicon;" the main facts of which correspond with my own experience. "In this degree, the Knights celebrate the destruction of the tower of Babel, and for this purpose they meet on the night of the full moon of each month. No other light is permitted in the Lodge than what proceeds from that satellite. The records of the order furnish us with the following history. The Noachites, at this day called Prussian Knights, are the descendants of Peleg, chief architect of the tower of Babel. Thus they trace the origin of their order to a more ancient date than the descendants of Hiram; for the tower of Babel was built many ages before the temple of Solomon. And formerly, it was not necessary that candidates for this degree should be Hiramites or Blue Masons. But a different regulation was afterwards adopted, and to receive the degree of Noachite, it is now necessary that the candidate should have performed the duties of a worthy office in a regularly-constituted Lodge of Blue Masons. The order of Noachites was established in Prussia in 1755, and introduced into France by the Count St Gelaire in 1757."

The degree of the Ark and Dove has also a reference to the deluge, and the eight persons saved in the ark, as its name imports; and describes the process by which Noah emerged from his confinement after the waters had subsided. There is still another degree which partially includes the same subject, only it confines its reference to the building of the ark. It is called the Knight of the Royal Axe; and by some the Grand Patriarch, Prince of Libanus, because the timber for the ark is feigned to have been felled in those extensive forests.

As I am on this subject, into which I have been insensibly led by its connection with the ogdoad, I may as well mention a tradition which is preserved in one of these degrees. It is there said, that " when Noah and his family entered into the ark, they assisted each other by means of a certain grip." There appears to be some doubt about the correctness of this tradition, which indeed is given by others in a different form. They say, that when the antediluvians underwent the divine sentence, and were struggling with the waves in the agony of death, they endeavoured to escape by using the same grip to pull each other up to the tops of mountains, or trees, or other high places that presented a temporary refuge from the justice of that irrevocable decree which brought destruction on their heads.

ANCIENT SUPERSTITIONS ATTACHED TO THE ENNEAD OR TRIPLE TRIANGLE.

THE TRIPLE TRIANGLE, ENNEAD, NONAGON, OR THE NUMBER NINE.

CHAPTER IX.

THE TRIPLE TRIANGLE.

ENNEAD, NONAGON, OR THE NUMBER NINE.

> "The weird sisters hand in hand,
> Posters of the sea and land,
> Thus do go about, about,
> Thrice to thine, and thrice to mine,
> And thrice again to make up nine."
> SHAKESPERE.

"THE emblems used to explain the number of the Nine Elected Knights were nine red roses, nine lights in the chapter, and nine strokes to gain admittance. The colour was symbolical of the blood that was shed in the temple, and ordered to remain there till revenge was completed."—LECTURE OF THE NINE ELECTED KNIGHTS.

THERE can be no doubt but the system of numerical cabalism, or divination by numbers, commonly called Arithomancy, may boast a very high antiquity. By which I mean, a system of foretelling remarkable events by the combinations of numbers according to the rules of art; and the results were sometimes so extraordinary as to startle the uninitiated.

Whether the sacred writings give any sanction to the practice is doubtful. The Jews assert that they do, and surely they ought to be the best interpreters of their own holy books. The learned critic and Hebraist, Dr Wootton, was of this opinion; and he thinks that we may safely receive their exposition when there is no reason to suspect any sectarian bias or prejudice in the mind of the commentator. Let them therefore answer the question about the cabalistic application of numbers in the interpretation of scripture, if they will—I shall not venture an opinion on the subject.

We are quite sure, however, that divination by numbers formed a part of the system of Pythagoras; for Stanley has given an entire chapter on the subject. He says, that Pythagoras derived his knowledge of the properties of numbers from Orpheus; and Iamblichus asserts, that instead of the art of divining by sacrifices, this philosopher taught the art of prediction by numbers; which he conceived to be more sacred and divine, and more agreeable to the celestial numbers of the gods. Some authors have ascribed to Pythagoras the invention of an onomantic kind of arithmetic, in which particular numbers are assigned to the letters of the alphabet, the planets, the signs of the zodiac, and the days of the week; thereby resolving questions concerning nativities, victory, journeys, thefts, prosperity or adversity, life or death. Dr Fludd, in his "Microcosm," affirms, that future events may be prognosticated by virtue of a wheel invented by Pythagoras, whereby everything connected with the life of man may be truly foretold. There are great doubts, however, whether this wheel was not an invention of the cabalists of an age long subsequent to the time of Pythagoras, because it is not mentioned by any ancient writer.

There is another method of using a combination of numbers to predicate or foretel remarkable events; although, from the specimens before us, they seem rather calculated, by an ingenious adaptation of facts to figures, to speculate on the past, rather than to vaticinate for the future. Thus we are told, that by selecting any remarkable year as the basis of the calculation, other coincident circumstances will be pointed out by adding the sum of the figures in them to the year itself. And this may be carried out *ad infinitum*; as in the following examples. The fall of Robespierre took place in the year 1794; now if the sum of 1, 7, 9, and 4, viz., 21, be added to that era, the result will give 1815, a year distinguished by the fall of Bonaparte; then add the sum of 1, 8, 1, and 5, viz., 15, to this latter year, and we have 1830, which was marked by the fall of Charles X.; and proceeding still further to add the sum of 1, 8, 3, and 0, viz., 12, to that year, it gives 1842, remarkable for the death of the Duke of Orleans. The same system has been applied to the House of Brunswick on the throne of England, with similar results. And it might be made to bear with a corresponding facility on any individual in the universe, taking the day of his birth for the era; and some prominent event will certainly mark every year which may be produced by the above process.

The ancients were much addicted to these puerilities, and considered every accidental coincidence as an extraordinary confirmation of a mystical or magical system. And so it has descended to our own times. Charms for curing diseases are not entirely obliterated; and a century or two ago they were abundantly prevalent amongst all ranks and descriptions of people; and every midwife was formally sworn before the civil magistrate, that in the discharge of her duties she will " use no kind of sorcery or incantation in the time of the travail of any woman." The charms which were in common use, most frequently combined the numeral system in one shape or other. For instance, the famous amulet, Abracadabra, contains an odd number of letters, viz., 11, for which number the Jews had a great veneration, because it reminded them of the bondage of their fathers in Egypt; there being only eleven patriarchs remaining when Joseph was transported thither and accounted dead; but some of the cabalistic Jews have given a more philosophical reason, by supposing that the solar exceeded the lunar year by so many days.

Again, the following charm " for woman that traveylyth of chylde," which was directed to be " byndyd to her thye," is founded on the numeral system, for almost all the invocations run by threes. "In Nomine Patris ✠ et Filii ✠ et Spiritus Sancti ✠ Amen. ✠ Per Virtutem Domini sint Medicina mei pia Crux et Passio Christi. ✠ Vulmera quinque Domini sint Medicina mei. ✠ Sancta Maria peperit Christum. ✠ Sancta Anna peperit Mariam. ✠ Sancta Elizabet peperit Johannem. ✠ Sancta Cecilia peperit Remigium.✠ Arepo tenet opera rotas. ✠ Christus vincit. ✠ Christus regnat. ✠ Christus dixit Lazare veni foras. ✠ Christus imperat. ✠ Christus te vocat. ✠ Mundus te gaudet. ✠ Lex te desiderat. ✠ Deus ultionum Dominus. ✠ Deus preliorum Dominus libera famulum tuam N. ✠ Dextra Domini fecit virtutem. a. g. l. a. ✠ Alpha ✠ et Ω. ✠ Anna peperit Mariam. ✠ Elizabet precursorem. ✠ Maria Dominum nostrum Jesum Christum, sine dolore et tristicia. O Infans sive vivus sive mortuus exi foras ✠ Christus te vocat ad lucem. ✠ Agyos. ✠ Agyos. ✠ Agyos. ✠ Christus vincit. ✠ Christus imperat. ✠ Christus regnat. ✠ Sanctus ✠ Sanctus ✠ Sanctus ✠ Dominus Deus. ✠ Christus qui es, qui eras, ✠ et qui venturus es. ✠ Amen. Churnon ✠ Clictaono ✠ Christus Nazarenus ✠ Rex Judeorum fili Dei ✠ miserere mei. ✠ Amen."

The Jewish purifications had an especial reference to the numbers 3, 7, and 9. For instance, a person who had been rendered unclean was sprinkled on the third and seventh day by a clean person with hyssop, dipped in water mixed with the ashes of a red heifer ritually prepared. Lightfoot informs us, that nine of these heifers were slain between the time of Moses and the destruction of the second temple.

Many learned and wise men amongst the ancients were fully persuaded that divination was a faculty which they themselves possessed, and it would be too much to charge so virtuous a philosopher as Pythagoras with the deliberate practice of imposture in his assumption of the power of foretelling future events. The truth is, he was himself deceived; and the fiction of having been taught the art by Orpheus and Aglaophemus, when he was initiated into the spurious Freemasonry of Thrace, as Iamblichus informs us, was as firmly implanted in his mind, as the faith of Socrates, that he was attended by a familiar demon, who, either openly or by the mediation of dreams and omens, communicated to him every important event of his life; forewarning him of danger, and frequently preventing him, by a timely admonition, from committing actions which he would afterwards have repented of.

All this was rejected by Epicurus. He allowed of no power either in oracles, dreams, or divination. He says, "They allege divination as an argument to prove both Providence and the existence of demons; but I am ashamed at human imbecility, when it fetcheth divinations even out of dreams; as if God, walking from bed to bed, did admonish supine persons, by indirect visions, what shall come to pass; and out of all kinds of portents and prodigies; as if chance were not a sufficient agent for these effects, but we must mix God, not only with the sun, the moon, and living creatures, but also with brass and stone. But to instance in oracles only. Many ways may it be evinced that they are mere impostures of priests, as may particularly be discovered, for that the verses which proceed from them are bad; being for the most part maimed in the beginning, imperfect in the middle, and lame in the close; which could not be if they came from divine inspiration; since from God nothing can proceed but what is decent and proper."[1]

The Ennead is the first square of an odd number, and possesses many curious properties. Thus, if we multiply 9 by itself, or by any other single figure, if we add the two figures of the product together, the sum in all cases will be 9. For example; 9 multiplied by 9 is 81; and 8 added to 1, make 9, and so with every other digit. Again, if all the nine digits be added together, the amount will be 45; and 4 added to 5 make 9. The amount of the several products of 9, viz., 9, 18, 27, 36, 45, 54, 63, 72, 81=405, when divided by 9 gives a quotient of 45, and the figures forming either the dividend or the quotient, added together, make 9. Again, if we multiply any row of figures either by 9, or by any of the above products of 9, the sum of the figures added together will be divisible by 9 without a remainder. And if we multiply the nine digits in

[1] Stanley, Hist. Phil., vol. iii. part 4, s. 2, c. 6.

their natural order by 9, or by any of the above products of 9, the result will come out all in the same figure except in the place of tens, which will be a 0; and that figure will be one, which, being multiplied by 9, supplies the multiplier; or in other words, if 9 be the multiplier, the product will be all ones; if 18, all twos; if 27, all threes; and if 8 be omitted from the multiplicand, the 0 will vanish, and leave the product all ones, twos, threes, &c., as the case may be. Once more, if a piece of square pasteboard be divided into nine cells, it has often exercised the ingenuity of curious persons to determine how the numbers 18, 20, 24, 28, 32, and 36 may be respectively placed in the outer cells of the squares, so as to form in every case the number 9, and no more, in each of the rows. The result is as follows :—

5		4
4		5

4	1	4
1		1
4	1	4

3	3	3
3		3
3	3	3

2	5	2
5		5
2	5	2

1	7	1
7		7
1	7	1

	9	
9		9
	9	

Another property of the number 9 is as follows: viz., take any number you choose, as, for

instance, 865374254
Invert their order and subtract them, 452473568
$$\overline{412900686}$$
then add together the figures in the last line, viz., $4+1+2+9+6+8+6=36$; and $3+6=9$. If the number in the uppermost line be smaller than the lower line, and cannot be subtracted from it, then take the top line from the bottom, and the result will be the same; as, for example,
1579
9571
$$\overline{7992}$$
and $7+9+9+2=27$, or thrice 9.

Amongst the heathen, the purification of male infants took place nine days after the birth; whence the goddess, who was supposed to preside over this ceremony, was called Nundina, from *nonus*, or the ninth; and for the same reason the Roman market-days were termed Nundinæ, Novendinæ, or Feriæ nundinales, because they were held every ninth day. The ennead had, however, a variety of other references, some of which are too curious to be passed over in silence.

It was called τελειος, or perfect, in reference to the time of gestation in the womb. And hence it is a custom of very ancient standing at marriages to put slices of bridecake through the wedding-ring nine times, and being thus invested with some supernatural power, the pieces are distributed amongst the young friends of the bride, that being laid under their pillows, they may have a dream or vision of the person who is designed to be their partner for life.

> With her own hand she charms the destin'd slice,
> And through the ring repeats the trebled thrice.
> The hallowed ring, infusing magic power,
> Bids Hymen's visions wait the midnight hour;
> The mystic treasure placed beneath her head,
> Will tell the fair if haply she may wed.

The number nine had the name of Likeness, because it is the first odd triangle; and Prometheus, because it is a perfect ternary; for he made the first man and woman, and animated them with fire from heaven. It was called Concord, because it unites and knits together all other numbers. It was considered to be unbounded, because, as we have just seen, in all its combinations it returns into itself; and therefore was compared equally with the horizon and the ocean; whence it was called $Εκαεργος$; for the ocean flowing about the habitable earth is believed by some to be so immediately placed under the arch of heaven, that the sun and stars rise from it, and set in it. And the Epicureans demonstrated the fact by this argument: "The universe consisting of vacuum and body is infinite; for that which is finite hath a bound, that which hath a bound is seen from some other thing; or may be seen from out of an interval beyond, or without it. But the universe is not seen out of any other things beyond it; for there is no interval or space which it containeth not within itself, otherwise it could not be an universe if it did not contain all space; therefore neither hath it any extremity. Now, that which hath no extremity hath no end, and that which hath no end doubtless is not finite but infinite. This is confirmed thus: If you imagine an extremity, and suppose some man placed in it who, with great force, throws a dart towards its utmost surface; the dart will either go forward or not. If it go forward, there is place beyond, wherefore the extremity was not there, where we designed it; if not, then there is something beyond which hinders the motion; and so, again, the extremity was not in the fore-designed place."[1]

The Pythagoreans gave the name of the number nine to several of the Grecian divinities,—as Juno, because the sphere of the air has the ninth place; and, like the ennead in its conjunction with unity, she was the sister and wife of Jupiter. It was also called Vulcan, for a reason which I do not well understand; Proserpine, because she presides over nine unpropitious deities; the three Fates, the three Furies, and Night, Sleep, and Death; Terpsichore, because the Muses are nine in number; and also Curetis, Pæan, Hyperion, Agelia, and many others; but I cannot ascertain any valid reason for each particular appropriation.

The Mahometans had ninety-nine names for the Deity; and the Jews believed that God had descended to the earth nine times; and that He shall come down on the tenth in the person of

[1] Stanley, Hist. Phil., vol. iii. part 4, p. 145.

the Messiah. His several appearances were—1, in the garden of Eden; 2, at the confusion of tongues; 3, at the destruction of Sodom; 4, to Moses at Mount Horeb; 5, at His appearance on Mount Sinai; 6 and 7, two other appearances to Moses; 8 and 9, in the Tabernacle.

There was at Cairo, during the dynasty of the Fatimite Khalifs, a secret society, called the Society of Wisdom. The members were clad in white, and held their meetings twice a week. The institution consisted of nine degrees: 1. Probation; in which the candidate was perplexed with abstruse questions, and taught to regard his teacher with veneration. 2. The Oath; and acknowledgment of the divine authority of the imams. 3. Instruction; principally consisting in a knowledge of mystical numbers; and particularly that seven was the noblest of God's creatures. 4. Illustrations of the number seven; in which he was taught, that as there were seven heavens, seven earths, the same number of seas, planets, metals, &c., so there were seven lawgivers, seven helpers, seven imams, &c. 5. Illustration of the number twelve. 6. The philosophy of religion. 7. Pantheism. 8. Scepticism. 9. This degree inculcated that nothing was to be believed, and that anything may be done; which, in point of fact, is Deism at the least, if not absolute Atheism.

The critical period of human life, according to a very ancient superstition, as we have already seen under the number seven, had a reference to this number. Thus 9 being multiplied by 7 makes 63, the climacteric or dangerous year; and 9 multiplied by 9 makes 81, the grand climacteric, or year of imminent danger. Levinus Lemnius thus accounts for the existence of the superstition. " Olde men," he says, " seldome passe their sixty-third year, but they are in constant danger of their lives; and I have observed in the Low Countries almost infinite examples thereof. Now there are two years, the seventh and ninth, that commonly bring great changes in a man's life, and great dangers; wherefore sixty-three, that containes both these numbers multiplied together, comes not without heapes of dangers; for nine times seven, or seven times nine, are sixty-three. And, thereupon, that is called the climactericall year; because, beginning from seven, it doth, as it were, by steps, finish a man's life."

I shall conclude this chapter with the mention of a few remarkable superstitions connected with the ennead, which will show the honours that were paid to it of olden time. It appears that in the time when conjurers could profitably exercise their art, they used to raise spirits within a circle nine feet in diameter, which they consecrated by sprinkling with a mixture of holy water, wine, and salt; that they might be protected from any onslaught of the fiend. Brand informs us, that it is unlucky to cut your nails upon a Friday or a Sunday; and that it ought to be done on the ninth day, except it fell on either of the above periods. This custom was used by the Romans.[1]

[1] Pop. Ant., vol. iii. p. 92.

Divination is sometimes practised by the use of this number, even at the present day. Thus, the female inquirer after a sight of the person to whom she is to be married is directed to beg nine keys of nine several persons; fastening them together by nine knots of a three-plaited braid of her own hair. She is then to tie them to her wrist at going to bed with one of her garters on St Peter's Eve, repeating—

> St Peter take it not amiss
> To try your favour I've done this;
> You are the ruler of the keys,
> Favour me then if you please;
> Let me then your influence prove,
> And see my dear and wedded love.

In divination, or fortune-telling by cards, the nine of spades is the most unfortunate in the whole pack; the nine of diamonds favourable to commercial men; the nine of clubs for married women; and the nine of hearts for lovers of either sex.

It would be easy to multiply instances of a superstitious affection for the number nine, but it is unnecessary, as the memory of every reader will be sufficiently retentive to suggest cases without end where it occurs. Our ancestors named nine worthies in triads; three being heathen, three Jewish, three Christian. The former were Hector, Alexander the Great, and Julius Cesar; the next, Joshua, David, and Judas Maccabeus; and the last, King Arthur of Britain, Charlemagne of France, and Godfrey de Bouillon, King of Jerusalem.

I am not aware of any reference to this number in symbolical Masonry, unless, with the cabalists, we consider it to be "the number evolving itself" in the consecutive reports of the principal officers of the Lodge, at opening, closing, and refreshment; but in the Royal Arch, and in the Ineffable Degrees, it is abundantly used. As, for instance, in the degree of Select Master, mention is made of a secret vault underground leading from King Solomon's most retired apartment westwardly, and consisting of nine separate apartments or arches, the latter being under the *Sanctum Sanctorum*. The method of giving and receiving the sacred word is ninefold; the arches of Enoch were nine in number; the Grand Masters of the three original Lodges were nine; and the symbolical ages of the members of different degrees were computed by the same number, as $27 = 3 \times 9$; $72 = 8 \times 9$; $81 = 9 \times 9$, &c.

These results are, I think, fatal to the theory which gives to Freemasonry an astronomical origin; because every rite and ceremony which may be presumed to bear the authentic stamp of antiquity is founded strictly on a reference to this number. The advocates for the astronomical tendency of Freemasonry thus state the grounds of their opinion, as appears from a letter to the author, written by a learned Scottish Mason. He says, " My conviction is, that the whole of Freemasonry is an astronomical allegory; for we cannot suppose that the wisest of men would suffer the Dionysian artificers to practise either their own impurities, or worship their false gods, in the Holy City. I think Faber has distinctly shown that the pagan mysteries refer to the Ark of Noah—to some one who was dead or killed, and again came to life—and that the rising and setting of the sun so aptly represented this person, that the type became subsequently worshipped for the substance. Moreover, all the ancient mysteries seem to have been celebrated about the time of the vernal equinox; and it is a general belief that King Solomon laid the foundation-stone of the Temple on the very same day. Now Josephus informs us, that the Tabernacle was a representation of the universe; which interpretation may also be applied to the Temple, because it was merely a renewal of the Tabernacle on a more magnificent scale. But the appearance of the heavens is continually changing; and therefore, if the above mean anything, the Temple must have represented the universe at the exact period of its erection. Although, then, the modern symbols may be derived from astronomy in imitation of the Egyptian Dionysiacs or Tsabaists, still we need no more admit them to be inseparable from the pagan idolatry, than that, as Solomon's Temple was itself an astronomical or universal emblem, Solomon had erected it for the rites of the pagans, instead of the worship of the only God. Why Solomon did permit such is not so clear, as that they must be viewed in themselves as having no tendency to idolatry, otherwise they could not have been allowed to be used. That afterwards Solomon and some of his successors blended the symbolic with the gross ritual of the Tsabaists is almost evident from several passages of the Bible; and it may have been after the reign of Josiah, or at the rebuilding by Zerubbabel, that the present tradition or legend of the Third Degree was drawn up; probably accidentally, from some traditional account of a riot by a few of the workmen to obtain the secret of a superior degree; and in which they confounded H.A.B. with Urim, literally Lights; but being plural, this was used for the great light, or the sun."

I have no room for a further statement of the theory which ascribes an astronomical origin to Freemasonry; but this will be sufficient to show the line of argument by which the hypothesis is attempted to be supported. I am persuaded, however, that the theory is erroneous, notwithstanding the great names by which it is upheld; amongst whom we find that of an eminent brother, Sir W. Drummond, the erudite author of the "Origines," from the perusal of which I have derived both amusement and instruction. It appears more probable that Freemasonry is an emanation from Geometry, which was indeed one of its primitive names; and the basis of Geometry is the science of Numbers, whose elements are the masonic point, line, superfice, and solid.

If, then, we turn our attention to Geometry, we shall find that it is the foundation of architecture, which we know was practised by the Tyrians and Dionysiacs at the building of Solomon's Temple;

and this is more than we can say for the knowledge of astronomy; for though it may be perfectly correct that the Tabernacle and Temple were emblems of the universe, yet this might be an allegorical conceit of the later Jews after the invention of the cabala; for Josephus lived at the very latest period of the Jewish polity, and witnessed the final destruction of the Temple by Titus. It is reasonable, therefore, to conclude, that Numbers, displayed in the science of geometry and applied to architecture, the rules of which are all founded on its principles, were the prototype and origin of the masonic science.

THE PERFECT NATURE OF THE DECAD OR CIRCLE, AND THE APPLICATION OF THE DODECAEDRON AS A REPRESENTATION OF THE SYSTEM OF THE UNIVERSE.

THE CIRCLE, DECAD, PANTELEIA, OR THE NUMBER TEN.

CHAPTER X.

THE CIRCLE.

DECAD, PANTELEIA, OR THE NUMBER TEN.

" Qui venit hic fluctus, fluctus supereminet omnes,
Posterior nono est, undecimoque prior."
OVID.

" A TRIANGLE with the Sun in the centre, its rays issuing forth to every point, is an emblem of the Deity, represented by a Circle, whose centre is everywhere, and circumference nowhere ; hereby denoting His omnipresence, and that all His attributes are perfection."—OLD R. A. LECTURES.

THERE is little benefit to be derived from Freemasonry in this Christian country, if it be divorced from all connection with the Christian religion ; although admitting that it would be a violation of the true principles of the Order to close our Lodges against the sincere professors of any other faith which includes the belief of one only God, the creator and governor of the world. And the framers of our lectures entertained the same opinion. At the present day, there are two classes amongst the fraternity who differ upon this point, although the difference is not very essential, or difficult to be reconciled. For this purpose a little discriminative arrangement is alone necessary. It is readily admitted that ancient Masonry *per se* might be intended as an universal institution, embracing all mankind who acknowledge and worship the Great Supreme. But the *Lectures of Masonry*, as they are at present constituted in this country, offer a modified view of the matter. They consist almost exclusively of a series of typical references to the Redeemer of mankind. Therefore, however the Christian Mason may be inclined to admit the application of Masonry to all existing religions, he cannot deny the facts contained in the lectures, without, at the same time, denying the veracity of the New Testament.

If a Christian brother admits that Freemasonry is a system of Light, and I think there scarcely exists a difference of opinion on the proposition, he must also believe the truth of the words so solemnly delivered by our venerable Grand Master St John the Evangelist, who, speaking of Christ, plainly says, "HE is the true Light, which lighteth every man that cometh into the world."[1] If, therefore, Masonry be a system of Light, and the Light be Christ, the unavoidable inference is, that Masonry is a branch of that universal religion which is destined, at some future period, to pervade the whole earth, as the waters cover the sea.

The great error of those who can find no

[1] John i. 9.

Christianity in Freemasonry is, the very superficial view which they take of our most holy faith. They restrict its operation to the last eighteen and a half centuries; whereas, if they believe the Scriptures, they would extend it back to the beginning of time, as St Paul instructs them to do. It is not to be wondered at that this error should be committed by a layman; but it is surprising that any Christian minister should exhibit such a total ignorance of the design of that gospel which he preaches every week of his life.

A talented American brother, the Rev. Salem Town, asserts, that " the principles of Speculative Freemasonry have the same co-eternal and unshaken foundation, contain and inculcate in substance the same truths, and propose the same ultimate end, as the doctrines of Christianity taught by divine revelation." And to prove that the Christian tendency of Freemasonry was an admitted dogma with our brethren of the last century, I subjoin an observation, which I have found amongst the MS. papers of my father, the late Rev. S. Oliver, under date of 1793: " Masonry, taken in any point of view, either pagan or Christian, human or divine, is far superior to every other institution known amongst men, and may, without impropriety, be termed the *Summum Bonum*, inasmuch as it contains the very essence of Christianity; and when used by the professors of any other faith, allures them to the practice of the most sublime Christian virtues, whilst they do not suspect that almost they have become Christians."

On the number ten the ancients were quite ecstatic both in their feelings and their written disquisitions. It represented Elysium, the abode of happy spirits. Like the Deity, it is a circle whose centre may be seen, but whose circumference is invisible. There is nothing beyond it. It formed, in the opinion of the ancients, the boundary and extent of every created thing. Would you count a greater number than it contains, you must recommence with unity, and go on till you are again stopped by the decad, and unity once more recurs.

What a sublime idea does this number present to our minds, when it refers us to boundless space! Worlds piled upon worlds at immeasurable distances from each other, all illuminated by their own suns; and myriads so far removed, that their light, though travelling for six thousand years, at the rate of twelve millions of miles in every minute of time, has not yet reached our globe. Herschel, with his forty-foot telescope, as Bro. Moran tells us in the *Freemason's Quarterly Review*, " could descry a cluster of stars consisting of 5000 individuals, 300,000 times deeper in space than Sirius probably is; or, to take a more distinct standard of comparison, if it were at the remoteness of 11,765,475,948,678,678,679 miles; or, in words, eleven millions seven hundred and sixty-five thousand four hundred and seventy-five billions, nine hundred and forty-eight thousand six hundred and seventy-eight millions, six hundred and seventy-eight thousand, six hundred and seventy-nine miles."[1]

If this immense space be the centre, where is the circumference? Bro. Moran advises, with great judgment, in the above exquisite paper (would that we had more of them!) · "Pause a moment, and imagine, if you can, what it is that the discoveries of Herschel have thus unfolded; a distance between this earth and the remotest visible system we behold with the unhelped eye, nine hundred times greater than that of the sun from the earth. Then bear in mind that such another system of stars is hung up in distant space, for no other object, at least as apparent to terrestrial man, than to serve as a specular resemblance of that which, until the other day, he fancied was infinite. It is thus only that we can conceive of the Great Architect of the Heavens, until the purification of death shall quicken the mortal conception."

Here, then, we have an apt illustration of the decad as the receptacle of all things. Hence it was called Universe and Sphere, because it included the number ten, viz., the earth, the seven planets, the heaven of fixed stars, and antichthon. It was also called *Kosmos*, or world, because the decad comprehends all numbers, as the world comprehends all forms. Thus Ecphantus, the Crotonian, who belonged to the school of Pythagoras, affirmed, "that the nature of every

[1] F. Q. R., 1837, p. 327, note.

P

animal is adapted to the world, and to the things contained in the world; because every animal thus conspiring, in union and consent, and having such a colligation of its parts, it follows a series which is most excellent, and at the same time necessary, through the attractive flux of the universe about it, which is effective of the general ornament of the world, and the peculiar permanency of everything which it contains. Hence it is called *Kosmos*, and is the most perfect of all animals."[1]

The decad was the great number of the Pythagoreans, because it comprehends all arithmetical and harmonical proportions. They deemed it to proceed from the diffusive nature of the triad, and its multiplying properties. Thus, if unity and duality be multiplied in this form, once twice 2 make 4, the sacred Tetractys, whence $1+2+3+4=10$. Now the half of 10 being 5, the middle number, if we take the next superior and the next inferior numbers 6 and 4, their sum will be 10; the next two in a similar progression, 7 and 3, will also make 10; and so on throughout the integers, *i.e.*, 8 and 2, and 9 and 1, produce the same result; and hence they called the number 10 the fountain of eternal nature, or God; His body Light, and His soul Truth. Numbers, they said, fall all under the monad; thus one monad is a monad; one duad is a duad, &c.; but the decad is the summary of number, which cannot be increased without returning to the monad.

[1] Taylor's Fragments, p. 27.

Goquet reduces the origin and use of this number to a very simple process. He says that it proceeds simply from counting the fingers; which were the first instruments used by men to assist them in the practice of numeration. Amongst the cabalistic Jews, 5, 6, and 10, were called circular numbers, for they argue, that as a person travelling on a circular road departs from a certain point, how often soever he goes round, he still returns to the same point; so is the property of numbers. If 1 be multiplied by 1, the result is one; 5 multiplied by 5 also gives a 5; 6 times 6, the same, and so on to infinity. The number 10 may thus be said to be circular; for, multiplied by itself, it is 100; and 10 times 100 are 1000, or 10 hundreds; thus showing, that as a circle has neither beginning nor end, so it is an apt symbol of the First Cause, who is without beginning and without end.

From this property of comprehending all number, the decad was called Power, for its command over all numbers; and also Atlas, because it sustains all the ten spheres of heaven, as Atlas bore the sphere of the universe upon his shoulders. St Thomas Aquinas, in his definition of quality or quantity compared with distance, has thus recorded his idea of the ten empyreal grades : " In our universe the water is more than the earth; the air more than the water; the fire more than the air; the first heaven is larger than the sphere of fire; the second larger than the first; and so on in regular gradation, until we arrive at the tenth sphere, which is *inestimabilis et incomparabilis magnitudinis.*"

The decad was also called Fulness and Eternity, by reason of its being the perfection of all number, and comprehending all the nature of odd and even, right and wrong, good and evil, light and darkness. Hence it was used by the Jewish prophets indefinitely for a great number. Thus, at the building of the Temple of Zerubbabel, Nehemiah interprets the ten generations mentioned in Deut. xxiii. 3, to mean "for ever;"[1] and speaking of Sanballat and his associates said, "It came to pass, that when the Jews which dwelt by them came, they said unto us ten times, from all places whence ye shall return unto us they will be upon you."[2] Meaning that they had *frequently* told them so. Moses Lowman, in his Commentary on the Book of Revelation, speaking of the ten-horned beast, says, that "ten, in prophetic language, does not always mean a precise number, but is used as a certain number for an uncertain, to express in general several or many; so that there seems no necessity of finding a precise number of ten different kingdoms erected on the ruins of the Roman Empire." Several interpreters, however, and amongst the rest Sir Isaac Newton, have enumerated these ten kingdoms.

The number ten had the further names of Sol, Urania, Memory, Necessity, and Faith; and was esteemed the first square, because it is composed

[1] Nehem. xiii. 1. [2] Ibid. iv. 12.

The Tenth Wave and Egg Ideas. 229

of the first four digits. Sir Isaac Newton, speaking on this subject, says that the extent of Solomon's Temple was 1460 cubits; but if we multiply this number by 4, and again by 365, the days in a solar year, it will give the exact area of the Temple, viz., the square of $1460 = 2,131,600$ cubits; thus practically illustrating the manner in which the Jewish cabalists combined the sciences of architecture and astronomy; for 1460 was the old Egyptian canicular year.

Of the number ten, Dr Brown says, "that *fluctus decumanus*, or the tenth wave, is greater and more dangerous than any other; some, no doubt, will be offended if we deny; which notwithstanding is evidently false; nor can it be made out by observation, either upon the shore or the ocean, as we have with diligence explored them both. Of affinity hereto is that conceit of *Ovum decumanum*—so called because the tenth egg is bigger than any other. For the honour we bear unto the clergy, we cannot but wish this were true; but herein will be found no more verity than in the other; and surely few will assent hereto without an implicit credulity, or Pythagorical submission unto every conception of number. For surely the conceit is numeral, and, though not in the sense apprehended, relateth unto the number of ten, as Franciscus Sylvius hath most probably declared. For whereas amongst simple numbers or digits, the number of ten is the greatest; therefore whatsoever was the greatest in every kind, might be in some sense named from this number."[1]

The foreign Masons of the last century, who called themselves Theosophists, or followers of Paracelsus, made use of this number in more than one of their high degrees. They taught, that as there were ten generations from Adam to Noah, ten from Shem to Abraham, and ten spiritual graces in Christianity, viz., love, joy, peace, long-suffering, gentleness, goodness, faith, prudence, meekness, and temperance;[2] so there are in nature ten forms of fire, which they enumerated, in imitation of the framers of the Royal Order of H.R.D.M., in doggrel rhyme:—

> Of the ten forms of fire know the skill,
> The *Liberty* both hath and is the will.
> Next *Strong desire*. Third, sharp drawing *Might*
> Makes an opposing will. Fourth, flash of *Light*
> Brings *Anguish*. And in the fifth form doth lie
> The *Eternal nature*, or Great Mystery.
> Sixth, the two principles of *Fire* and *Light*,
> The seventh *Magia* with reflecting sight.
> The eighth with *Turba* ends the outward life.
> Ninth *Virgin tincture* pacifying strife.
> The tenth makes holy flesh and holy earth,
> Of *Angels* and blest souls, the holy birth.

The theological ladder, which Masons make to consist of three rounds, referring to Faith, Hope, and Charity, the Jewish cabalists increased to seven, and subsequently to ten principal steps, called the seven divine splendours, which were

---

[1] Pseudo. Epidem., p. 404.   [2] See Gal. v. 22.

surmounted by the three great hypostases of the Deity; which they made figuratively to penetrate the heavens, which were represented by the number ten ; and, in consequence of the perfection of that number, they crowned the symbol with a nimbus to represent the throne of the Most High.

It has several times been remarked in the course of these numeral dissertations, that the true religion, under the Mosaic dispensation, had an appointed reference to particular numbers. The facts have been briefly stated under each several head ; but they are too extensive to be wholly included in my plan. This extraordinary fact still forms a part of Jewish ceremony. A congregation with them consists of ten persons ; and a less number would not make one. And we are told that, formerly, wherever ten Jewish families were resident in the same place; they were obliged to build a synagogue. At marriages, the bridegroom received seven blessings, which could not be pronounced except in the presence of ten persons. Again, the Jewish doctors hold that Abraham's faith and obedience were ten times tried, viz., 1, in quitting his native country ; 2, his flight to Egypt from the famine of Canaan ; 3, the first seizure of Sarah in Egypt ; 4, the war for the rescue of Lot ; 5, his taking Hagar at the request of Sarah ; 6, his circumcision ; 7, the second seizure of Sarah in Gerar ; 8, the expulsion of Ishmael ; 9, the expulsion of Hagar ; 10, the offering of Isaac.

And again, with respect to the number 12. The sons of Ishmael and Jacob were alike twelve in number, the latter of whom formed the heads of the house of Israel. The table of shewbread was directed by God himself to be furnished with twelve loaves; and the offering of the princes at the dedication of the altars, amongst other things, was twelve golden spoons or censers for incense. Joshua set up twelve stones in Jordan; respecting which an old masonic formula in my possession, has the following illustration: "As Joshua was conducting the Israelites towards the Promised Land, a remarkable miracle was performed in behalf of this people at the passing of the river Jordan. When the priests who bore the ark came near the narrow bridge, which would have been extremely incommodious for so large a body of people to pass, the waters of the river miraculously separated, as they had done before at the passage of the Red Sea, and left the bed of the river for a considerable breadth perfectly dry, so that the Israelites might pass over, with their families and cattle, without the slightest obstruction. In commemoration of this extraordinary interposition of the Most High in their behalf, Joshua commanded that twelve of the largest stones that could be found should be taken from the foundation on the north side of the bridge, and deposited in the adjoining field of corn, as the basis of a pillar, which was intended to be a memorial of this event; and that twelve similar stones should be collected from the country on the opposite side of the river, and placed in the situation from whence the other twelve were taken, to form the basis of another pillar in the river. These two pillars were solemnly dedicated by Joshua to ELELOHE ISRAEL, or God of Israel; and together they formed a subject of disquisition with our ancient brethren, which excited much attention in the Lodges."

But to return to the application of the number twelve in the Jewish scriptures. The chief officers of Solomon's household were twelve; the pillars of the porch were twelve cubits in circumference; the molten sea was supported by twelve oxen; and the steps of Solomon's throne were flanked by twelve lions. In the temple described by Ezekiel, the altar was directed to be twelve cubits square.

In Christian symbolism, the imagery was the same, and had a particular allusion to this number, formed out of the two perfect numbers, the triad and tetrad; thus $3 \times 4 = 12$. Jesus Christ was taken by His parents to keep the Feast of the Passover when He was twelve years old; and He chose for His companions twelve men whom He taught His doctrines, and sent forth to preach the everlasting gospel to mankind. In the Apocalypse, we have a glorious figure which includes this number: "There appeared a great wonder in heaven; a woman clothed with the Sun, and the Moon under her feet, and upon her head a crown of twelve Stars." This refers to the primitive Apostolic Church before the apostasy; where being clothed with the Sun, signifies her being environed with the pure light of the gospel, or the Sun of Righteousness communicated to her. And her being crowned with twelve Stars denotes, that it was her glory, and her crown, that she had not degenerated from the true Apostolic faith and practice."[1]

The new Jerusalem is represented as being accessible by twelve gates, disposed in conformity with the cardinal points of the compass; and those that were accounted worthy to be admitted into the holy city, were sealed in their foreheads; viz., of each of the tribes twelve thousand; which, as Dr More observes, " is not numerally to be understood, but symbolically, noting the condition of the sealed. And there were sealed an hundred and forty-four thousand; which chiliads or thousands are cubical numbers, and signify therefore stability or constancy. But it is said there were 144,000, it being the square number of these chiliads or companies, of which the root is twelve, the Apostolical number. Of all the tribes of the children of Israel, viz., the twelve patriarchs typically or figuratively being put for the twelve Apostles, and the children of Israel for the Church of Christ, of which the Israelites are a type, as they are in the Epistle to the Church in Pergamus, in which Pergamenian interval this sealing begins."[2]

[1] More, Apocalypsis, p 114.   [2] Ibid., p. 63.

It is the opinion of Mr Faber, whose learning and extensive researches into the hidden mysteries of antiquity are entitled to universal respect, that in the Book of Revelation "an important prophecy is most curiously and artfully veiled under the very language and imagery of the Orgies. To the sea-born Great Father was ascribed a threefold state: he lived, he died, and he revived; and these changes of condition were duly exhibited in the mysteries. To the sea-born wild beast is similarly ascribed a threefold state: he lives, he dies, and he revives. While dead, he lies floating on the mighty ocean, just like Horus, or Osiris, Siva, or Vishnu; when he revives, again like those kindred deities, he emerges from the waves; and whether dead or alive, he bears seven heads and ten horns, corresponding in number with the seven art-preserved Rishis, and the ten aboriginal patriarchs. Nor is this all; as the worshippers of the Great Father bore his special mark or stigma, and were distinguished by his name, so the worshippers of the maritime beast equally bear his mark, and are equally designated by his appellation."[1]

If this be true, and the arguments adduced in its support appear sound and conclusive, the above mystical ceremony of sealing the redeemed may be taken from the custom of marking the aspirant with a permanent badge of initiation, which may be an indelible token of his acceptance.

[1] Fab. Pag. Idol., vol. iii. p. 643.

Printed in Great Britain
by Amazon